Introduction to Generative AI with Julia and Python

From Theory to Practice

Pierluigi Riti

Apress®

Introduction to Generative AI with Julia and Python: From Theory to Practice

Pierluigi Riti
Mullingar, Westmeath, Ireland

ISBN-13 (pbk): 979-8-8688-2328-2 ISBN-13 (electronic): 979-8-8688-2329-9
https://doi.org/10.1007/979-8-8688-2329-9

Managing Director, Apress Media LLC: Welmoed Spahr
Acquisitions Editor: Melissa Duffy
Development Editor: James Markham
Copy Editor: Kezia Endsley
Editorial Assistant: Gryffin Winkler

Cover designed by eStudioCalamar

Cover Photo by Dim Gunger on Unsplash.com

Distributed to the book trade worldwide by Springer Science+Business Media New York, 1 New York Plaza, New York, NY 10004. Phone 1-800-SPRINGER, fax (201) 348-4505, e-mail orders-ny@springer-sbm.com, or visit www.springeronline.com. Apress Media, LLC is a Delaware LLC and the sole member (owner) is Springer Science + Business Media Finance Inc (SSBM Finance Inc). SSBM Finance Inc is a **Delaware** corporation.

For information on translations, please e-mail booktranslations@springernature.com; for reprint, paperback, or audio rights, please e-mail bookpermissions@springernature.com.

Apress titles may be purchased in bulk for academic, corporate, or promotional use. eBook versions and licenses are also available for most titles. For more information, reference our Print and eBook Bulk Sales web page at http://www.apress.com/bulk-sales.

Any source code or other supplementary material referenced by the author in this book is available to readers on GitHub. For more detailed information, please visit https://www.apress.com/gp/services/source-code.

If disposing of this product, please recycle the paper

To my family.

Table of Contents

About the Author

Pierluigi Riti is currently a technical leader with Mastercard. Before that, he was a senior software engineer at Coupa, Synchronos, Ericsson, and Tata. His experience includes designing and implementing complex software architectures. He also has over 20 years of experience in general design and development of applications at different scales, particularly in the telco and financial industries. Pierluigi holds a Master's degree in Science of Artificial Intelligence from the University of Limerick and is a researcher with South-East Technological University in Ireland, focusing on high-tech startups in the field of AI.

About the Technical Reviewer

Mohit Taneja is an AI humanist and currently works as an AI Engineering Manager at Workhuman, with over a decade of experience building scalable, human-centric AI products. At Workhuman, he leads cross-functional teams developing AI-driven solutions that elevate workplace engagement and empower people. His background spans industry, research, and academia, bringing together deep technical expertise, product thinking, and a commitment to responsible innovation. Previously at Mastercard, Mohit led multiple AI and Generative AI initiatives, contributing 14 invention disclosures and 12 patent applications. He has also lectured in computing and conducted research at the Walton Institute and CONNECT Centre, focusing on AI, IoT, and distributed systems.

Driven by the belief that technology should meaningfully serve people, Mohit focuses on the intersection of AI, business value, and human impact—building systems that solve complex challenges and create lasting global change.

Introduction

This book explains what *generative artificial intelligence* (GenAI) is, which is not a passing trend. It's a technology that has come to stay. If you ask to someone for an example of GenAI, they might mention ChatGPT, Gemini, Claude, or any other Large Language Model (LLM), which are very good examples. However, the field is much bigger than that.

This book presents different uses of the GenAI, including generative adversarial networks, autoencoders, and variational-autoencoders. You will learn how these models learn and reproduce the data. This book also explains how to use Python and Julia to code for different flavors of the same architecture.

Every chapter is mixed with theory and practice, which will give you the basics to expand your knowledge and improve your skill. The book is not intended to explain the entire topic, but to be an introduction that you can use to improve and start your own journey in the field of the GenAI.

Artificial Intelligence: A Gentle Introduction

We live in an interesting era. We are witnessing the rise of artificial intelligence and all the new opportunities it has created. However, to get the best results from these opportunities, we need to learn new skills and acquire knowledge.

This book explains the field of *generative artificial intelligence* (GenAI). This is one of the most interesting fields to be in. The book explains the basic theory and covers some practical examples. This type of combined work will help you understand the concepts behind some well-known AI models, including ChatGPT, Hugging Face, and DALL-E.

This chapter introduces the basic science of artificial intelligence, which in my opinion is one of the most exciting sub-fields of computer science. You can use this information as a foundation for understanding the differences between artificial intelligence, machine learning, and deep learning.

What Is Artificial Intelligence?

Nowadays it is not difficult to hear something new about artificial intelligence, such as a new AI model or application. If you are curious like me, you probably start to ask yourself, what is artificial intelligence? What is the difference between artificial intelligence and machine learning?

The first step is to define "artificial intelligence". This definition is based on an Alan Tuning article published in the 1950s called "Computing and Machinery Intelligence," which states:

> *The science and engineering of making computer machines able to perform a task that normally requires human intelligence.*

© Pierluigi Riti 2026
P. Riti, *Introduction to Generative AI with Julia and Python*, https://doi.org/10.1007/979-8-8688-2329-9_1

Based on this definition, we can see that artificial intelligence is a science. This is the first difference between machine learning and artificial intelligence. Machine learning is defined this way:

The field of study in artificial intelligence that explores the use of statistical algorithms that can learn from data.

The last term we need to define is deep learning. Deep learning is defined this way:

A sub-field of machine learning based on the use of artificial neural networks for learning and identifying the underlying patterns in data.

As you can see from the definition, artificial intelligence is the science. The application of the science is machine learning or deep learning. They have in common the use of data, which is used to learn how the "problem" is defined and how to solve it. Figure 1-1 shows a graphical representation of the science of artificial intelligence and its sub-fields.

When you hear about a new artificial intelligence model developed by some organization, they probably are referring to a new machine learning or deep learning model that's designed to solve a specific problem, which is solved *by learning from the data*.

This is important to remember when we talk about machine learning or deep learning. We always talk about a statistical or probabilistic algorithm that learns the underlying pattern of the data. This technology does not have any critical thinking capacity.

The first discipline you need to learn about is machine learning. It gives you the foundation for better understanding *generative artificial intelligence*. Or, better termed as *generative deep learning*. Because artificial intelligence is the name of the science, while deep learning is the application of the science itself.

I use the term "Generative AI" or "Generative Artificial Intelligence" in this book, because this is the term used in the outside world. But in reality, the model you create is a deep learning model, as you will soon see.

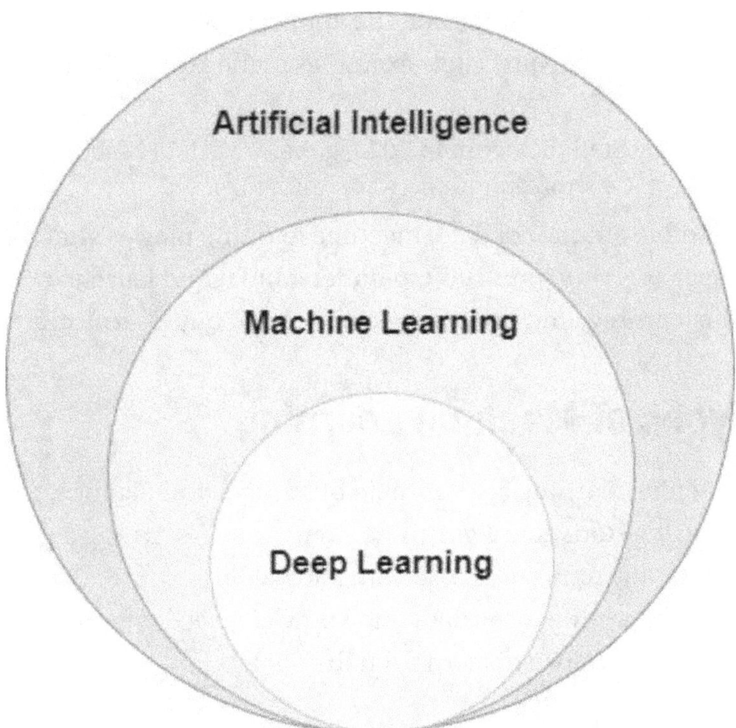

Figure 1-1. *The relationship between artificial intelligence, machine learning, and deep learning*

Machine Learning: Teaching a Machine to Learn

Machine learning was the first implementation of the science of artificial intelligence.

Machine learning comes directly from the article published by Alan Turing. It is the use of statistics to allow a computer (a "machine") to learn from the data. This is probably one of the most interesting fields to be in at this stage. If you imagine yourself in the future looking back at this time, you can easily say this is the start of the "age of the data".

Every day people produce and consume trillions of data. Consider your daily routine. You wake up and your mobile phone downloads your emails. Maybe you listen to some music on Spotify or browse the Internet. You read your favorite online newspaper. Your kids watch YouTube videos or a cartoon from a streaming platform during breakfast. You get a coffee at your favorite place on the way to work, pay with a debit card, and possibly use your fidelity card to collect points. If you need directions to somewhere, you just put the address into Google Maps and the application finds the best journey based on your preferences. These are just a few examples of the kinds of data people generate every day.

Based on a study by Statistica.com in 2020, generated data reached 64.2 zettabytes, and the site forecasted over 180 zettabytes generated by 2025.

With this incredible amount of data, machine learning plays a vital role in our daily lives. As an engineer, it is very important to understand it and learn to use it. But what exactly is machine learning, and how many types of machine learning are there?

Different Types of Machine Learning

As mentioned, machine learning is a sub-field of artificial intelligence. So, it is a science. It is the science of using statistical algorithms to create self-learning algorithms. These algorithms learn from the data and turn it into knowledge.

The way machine learning turns data into knowledge is the interesting part. There are three categories you can use to learn from the data:

- Supervised learning

- Unsupervised learning

- Reinforcement learning

Each category is designed to solve a specific class of problems. Because of that, they use specific algorithms to solve their problems.

Note that I don't mention deep learning or the artificial neural network here, because they are more architecture than a specific set of algorithms. The section describes the basics of machine learning as a foundation to build the rest of the knowledge.

Supervised Learning: Learning from Labelled Data

Supervised learning is a model that learns from labelled data. The algorithm learns the underlying data's pattern using labelled data.

After learning the main characteristics of the data's main features, it applies the same knowledge to unseen data.

Supervised learning has these specific characteristics:

- The algorithm is fed with labelled data

- There is direct feedback about the data

- The algorithm can predict the outcome of the unseen data

To illustrate how supervised learning works, Figure 1-2 shows a 10,000-foot overview. The labelled data used for the training, in this case, the image of the different dogs, is fed to the machine learning model.

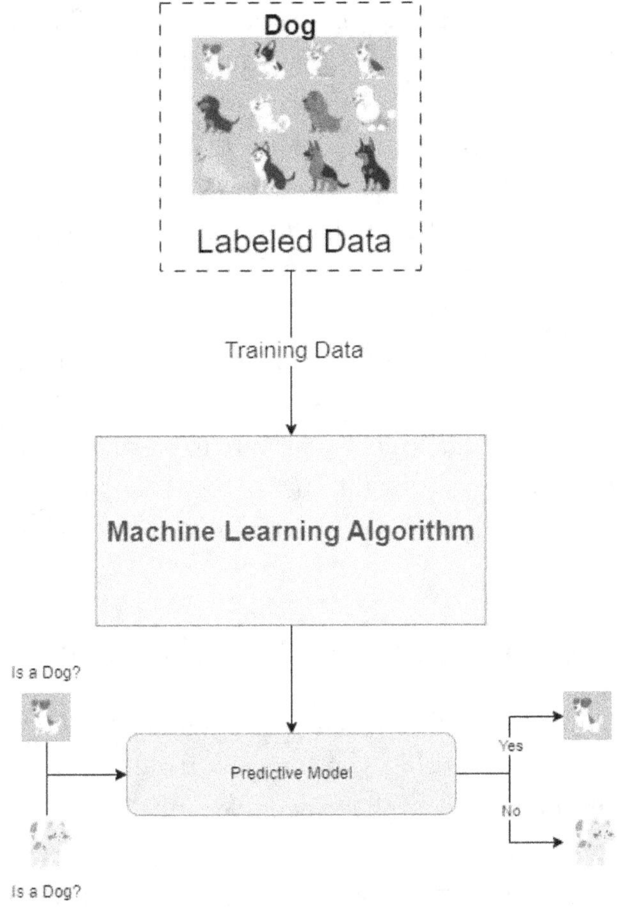

Figure 1-2. *An overview of a supervised learning model*

The model learns the specific characteristics of the dogs and then, as a result, you get a predictive model.

This is the result of the training done by the machine learning algorithm on the labelled data. With the model trained, you can make predictions on the unseen data. For example, if you were to try to classify a picture of a golden retriever as a dog or a cat, the model would correctly classify it as a dog.

The main goal of a *classification algorithm* is to predict the categorical class of unlabeled data. The model does this by learning the fundamental structure of past data. In this example, that's the training data.

This previous example—the cat and the dog—is called *binary classification*. The algorithm learns how to classify one type of data. However, classification can also be used for multiple types of data, which is called *multiclass classification*. The labelled data represents different types of data. One example is the classification of a handwritten digit. The MINST dataset contains different digits, 0 to 9. The algorithm will learn to recognize each digit and then properly classify any digit between 0 and 9.

Another type of classification is called *regression analysis*. In this type of analysis, there are several *explanatory variables*, called *features* in the field of machine learning, as well as continuous response *outcome variables*, called *target variables* in the field of machine learning. The goal of the algorithm is to find a correlation between the explanatory variables and the outcome variables so it can predict the outcome from unseen data.

Regression can be used, for example, if you want to predict the price of a house. Imagine that you want to know how the number of rooms and the square feet influence the price of a home in your town. When you train the algorithm, you can use it to predict the outcome of new data.

Unsupervised Learning: Discover Hidden Information in the Data

Supervised learning uses labelled data to learn the main features of the data and predict the outcome. In unsupervised learning, you can extract meaningful information without any previous knowledge of the data or the expected results.

In supervised learning, you know the label. But, in unsupervised learning, you have no idea about the data. In unsupervised learning, you classify through *clustering*.

Clustering is a type of exploratory data analysis (EDA). Its main goal is to group the data based on common characteristics. The different types of groups are called *clusters*. Each object in a cluster is similar. By the same token, they are less similar to objects in other clusters.

Figure 1-3 shows a visual example of clustering. The two clusters show dogs and cats. The data in the cluster is split based on the features of X_1 and X_2.

Figure 1-3. *An example of clustering*

Figure 1-4 shows an example of how a machine learning model for clustering works. The inputs are all unlabeled. The model identifies the unique features of the object and creates the cluster based on similarities. It creates the clusters based on major similarities.

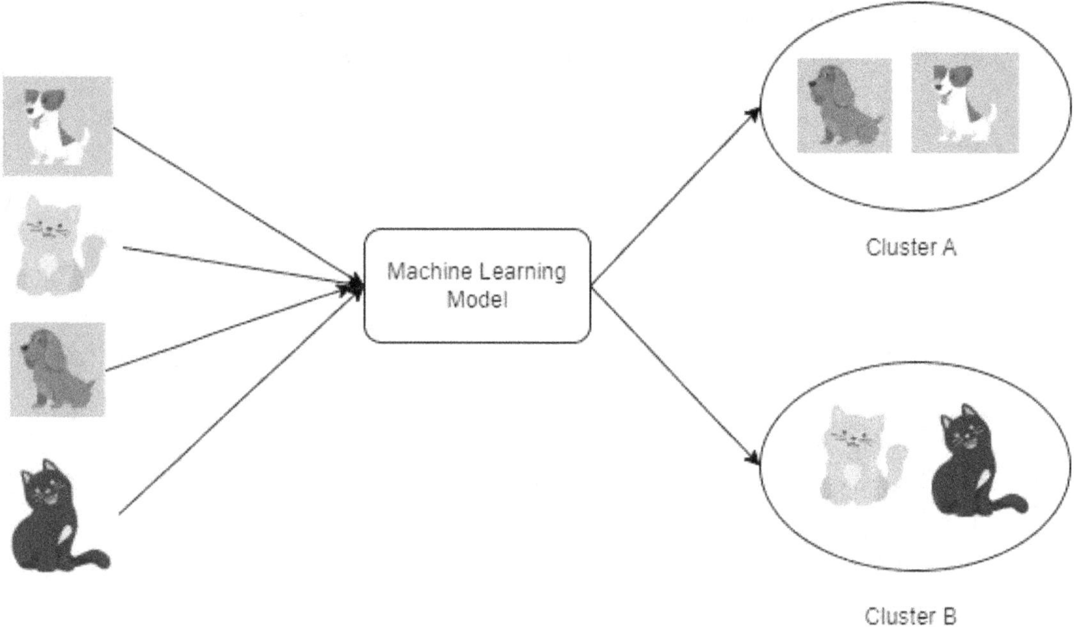

Figure 1-4. *An example of clustering workflow*

Another unsupervised learning technique is called *dimensionality reduction.* It is commonly used when you need to preprocess data to reduce its noise. Removing the noise from data is important. For example, removing the outliers increases any predictive information.

Reinforcement Learning: Learning from Errors

Reinforcement learning is another type of machine learning. This technique is most similar to the way humans learn.

Reinforcement learning's goal is to make the *agent* learn by interacting with the system. The interaction between the agent and the system produces a *reward*. The agent uses this reward to enhance the interactions and achieve the goal.

The agent can learn in two ways. One way is via *exploratory approaches,* where the agent explores the entire system before making a decision. The other way is through the *trial-and-error approach,* where every action made by the agent will return a positive or negative response.

The final goal of a reinforcement learning model is to maximize the reward. This type of machine learning had a huge impact on the development and creation of generative deep learning applications. The most commonly known example of this is ChatGPT.

There are different subtypes of reinforcement learning, but in general, the reinforcement learning schema can be defined similar to what is shown in Figure 1-5. An agent executes an action on the environment; it then receives a new state and the reward connected to the action.

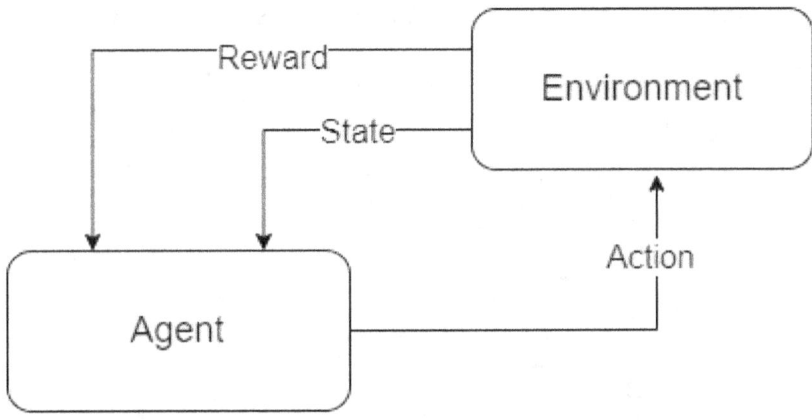

Figure 1-5. *A schema that represents the reinforcement learning method*

One difference between reinforcement learning and the other machine learning methodologies is the goal of a reinforced learning algorithm.

In reinforcement learning, the only concern is identifying the set of actions that maximize the total reward. This reward could be earned by an immediate action or via *delayed* feedback. You use reinforced learning when you want to create a system that can learn by specific actions.

The capacity to get a reward via delayed feedback is important when we talk about the architecture behind the famous OpenAI software ChatGPT. This model uses *reinforcement learning from human feedback,* RLHF. In this type of architecture, the agent gets delayed feedback from the human. In this case, the human can provide a different reward to the action chosen by the model and the model will improve the action in order to maximize the reward.

Artificial Neural Network: The Emulation of a Human Neuron

Machine learning and artificial intelligence science can be related to the 1943 paper published by Warren McCulloch and Walter Pitts.

In the paper "A Logical Calculus of the Ideas in Immanent in Nervous Activity," they describe the concept that simplifies the brain cells. Because of their paper, this neuron was named *McCulloch-Pitts Neuron,* or MCP. Figure 1-6 shows a representation of a brain neuron.

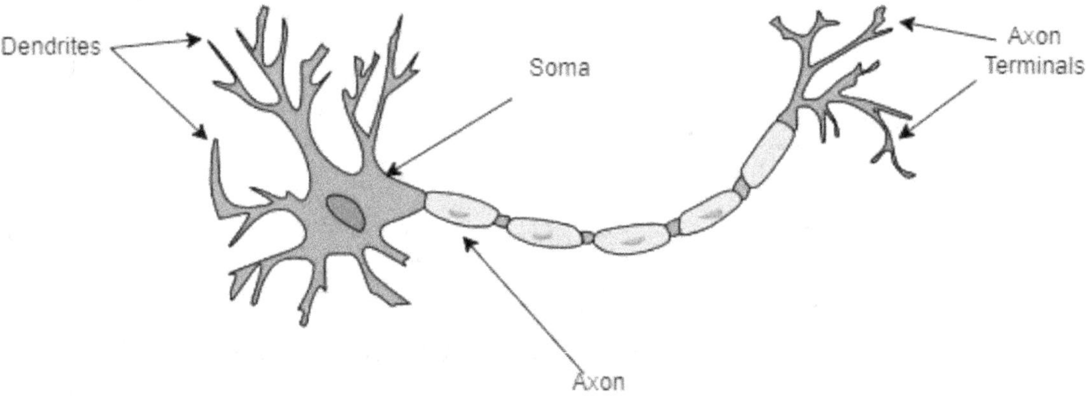

Figure 1-6. *A schema of a brain neuron*

McCulloch and Pitts compare this basic nerve cell to a logical gate. The dendrites receive multiple inputs, accumulate them, and when they reach a certain threshold, output is made. The output is sent out through the axon to the axon terminals.

In 1957, Frank Rosenblatt published the paper "The Perceptron: A Perceiving and Recognizing Automation." In it, he described the perceptron rule as an algorithm. This algorithm learns the input to determine if it fires the signal or not. Figure 1-7 shows a simple schema of a perceptron.

Rosenblatt proposed the basic perceptron. It sees the neuron as a simple logical gate. The inputs are weighed because not all the information has the same value. To show this difference, the inputs have different weights.

The sum of all the inputs is sent to the threshold function. This function "activates" the input and predicts the output based on the result.

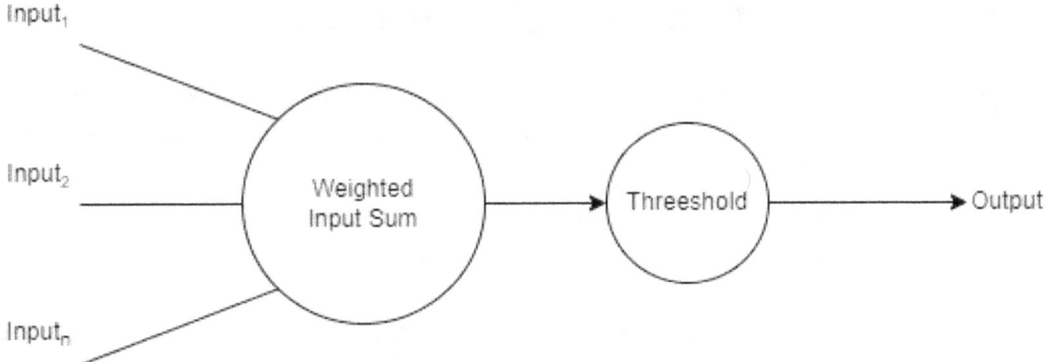

Figure 1-7. A schema of a perceptron based on the Rosenblatt definition

The basic perceptron is the core of the artificial neural network. In classification and prediction, this algorithm determines if the point belongs to a specific class or not.

The Perceptron Formula

To better understand how a perceptron works, this section formally describes it. This can help you understand the idea behind artificial neurons and how they can be put together to build a more complex neural network.

In the simplest context, binary classification, the perceptron uses the input to calculate the output. It gives 1 for the positive class and -1 for the negative class.

As you can see in Figure 1-7, the perceptron adds the weighted input sum. This is essentially a *linear combination* of the input values (x) and their weight (w). The result is the net-input (z). The mathematical formula can be represented in this way:

$$z = w_1 x_1 + w_2 x_2 + \ldots + w_n x_n = w^T x$$

If the result of the net input for the xis_n if less than the threshold, indicated by the Greek letter theta, θ, the class will have a value of 1. If the threshold is lower, the value will be -1.

The goal of the book is to give you practical examples of how to develop machine learning and deep learning models. To that end, the next section moves from the simple perceptron formula to real code implementation. This example uses pure Python and Julia.

Implementing a Basic Perceptron with Python

This section shows how to create a very basic perceptron. It's essentially a single-neuron neural network. This neuron can make "decisions" based on the input. It is a simple form of machine learning.

The perceptron designed by Rosenblatt has some basic components that you can easily replicate. Listing 1-1 shows a simple perceptron using pure Python.

Listing 1-1. An Example of a Perceptron in Pure Python

```python
import math

x = [1, 2.1, 1.4, 1.5] # position 0 is the bias the value is 1
W = [0.1, 0.3, 0.2, 0.5] #the weight associated with the input
z = .0

def network_input(x, W):
    net_value = .0
    for i in range(len(x)):
        net_value += x[i]*W[i]

    return net_value

def sigmoid(z):
    sigmoid_value = 1.0/(1.0 + math.exp(-z))

    return sigmoid_value

def logistic_activation(w, X):
    z = network_input(w,X)

    return sigmoid(z)


if __name__ == '__main__':
    print('P(y=1|x) = %.3f' % logistic_activation(x,W))
```

Listing 1-1 shows a simple perceptron. The first function is network_input(x, W). It calculates the net input based on the Rosenblatt perceptron. This is the dot product of the two vectors: the weight and the input.

The dot product is a simple linear algebra operation. You multiply the ith element of one array by the other one. Because it's a sum, you need to add the value calculated for the n-iteration to the previous one. The mathematical formula is as follows:

$$\sum_{i=1}^{n} x_i w_i$$

In pure Python, you can write the equation with this code:

```
net_value = .0
for i in range(len(x)):
    net_value += x[i]*W[i]
```

You essentially create the net_value variable, initialized with the value .0, which makes Python create a float number.

The sum of the value is calculated inside the for loop. It multiplies the value of the element i of the two arrays and adds it to the previous net_value.

Another key function of a perceptron is an *activation function*. There are different types of this function. The goal of this function is to elaborate the net_value and decide whether the neuron should be activated or not.

There are many types of activation functions, a few of which are Sigmoid, tanh, ReLU, Leaky ReLU, and Softmax. This example uses the simplest one (Sigmoid) and you will see other activation functions later in the book.

The activation function used in this example is called *Sigmoid*. The Sigmoid function is an s-shaped curve. The mathematical definition of the Sigmoid function is as follows:

$$\sigma(z) = \frac{1}{1 + e^{-z}}$$

Where e is the Euler constant. The reason for using the Sigmoid function is that the value can only be between 0 and 1.

Because of that, the function can predict the probability as output. In machine learning, this is translated to the confidence of the class that you want to classify.

In the code, `sigmoid(z)` re-creates the mathematical formula for the Sigmoid activation function. The code is quite simple:

```
sigmoid_value = 1.0/(1.0 + math.exp(-z))
```

This simple line represents the Python translation of the Sigmoid formula.

With the activation formula defined, you can finally call the perceptron and execute it. The execution is made by the `logistic_activation(w, X)` function. The perceptron returns the value based on the probability. The probability is based on the value of the two arrays, *w* and *X*. In this case, this is the value:

```
P(y=1|x) = 0.853
```

This is a very basic artificial neural network. It only uses one neuron. But the code also has a huge limitation. It can't learn because it doesn't encounter any errors in the decision process.

Errors are the key to learning in the perceptron. When it encounters errors, it updates the value of the weight to better fit the data's underlying function.

You will see the use of errors and their importance when I describe more complex algorithms. For now, I want to give you the basic idea of machine learning and its components.

Deep Learning Emulates the Human Brain

Deep learning is one of the most advanced architectures for machine learning. Deep learning is an evolution of the artificial neural network.

Deep learning architectures use a *multi-layer perceptron (MLP)* to find patterns in unstructured data. Figure 1-8 shows an MLP.

An MLP has many layers of perceptrons. The perceptrons are all connected, and the first layer is called the *input layer*. The input layer is connected to the *hidden layer*. The connection between the layers is only *forward*.

This type of architecture is called a *feedforward network*. In this type of architecture, the output of the first layer is sent as input to the subsequent layer. This structure allows you to work with more complex, unstructured data.

Working with unstructured data enables deep learning and MLP to work with non-tabular data.

This is a huge difference between deep learning and machine learning algorithms. An example of unstructured data is an image. The algorithm can classify a picture because a brown pixel is near a white one.

However, different layers learn specific information about the data. For example, they can learn the edge of the image, and then use the knowledge to classify better.

Unstructured data refers to any type of data that can be represented in a tabular way, such as images, text, and audio.

Because deep learning is essentially a set of layers, it's sometimes defined as a *deep neural network*. To understand how deep neural networks work, let's look at how it makes a classification. As shown in Figure 1-8, a deep neural network has a stack of *layers*. The first layer is the input. Each *unit* in the layer, a single perceptron, is connected to the other units of the deepest layer.

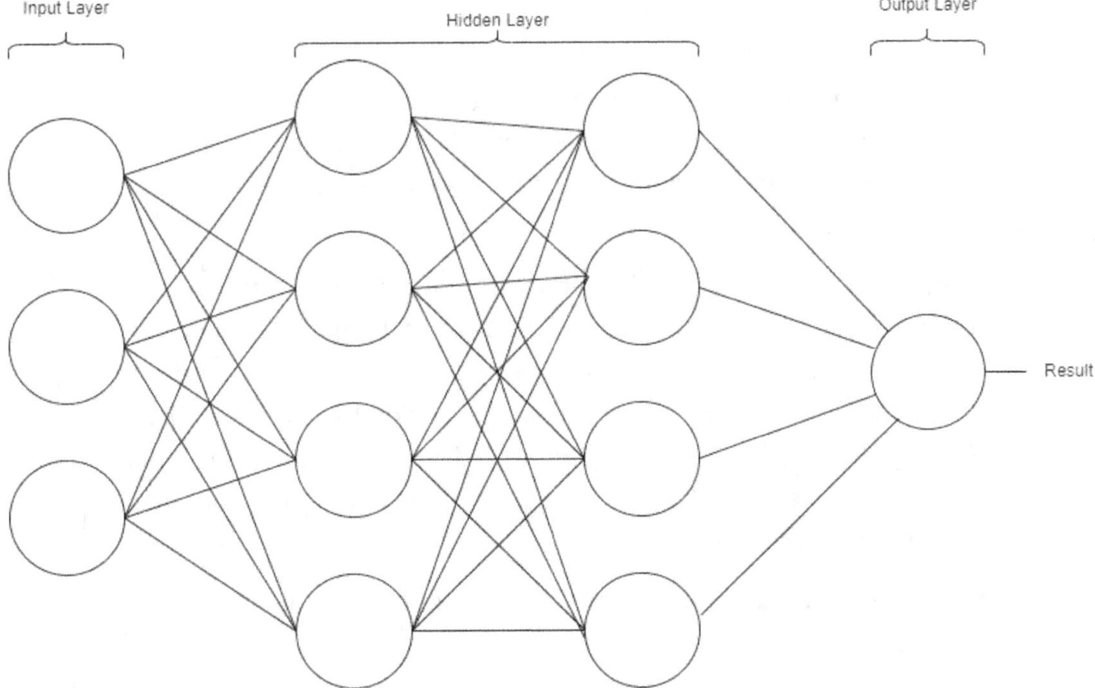

Figure 1-8. *The multi-layer perceptron architecture*

The connection is made using the output of the previous unit as a *weight* for the next unit. In the example shown in Figure 1-8, the layer is defined as a *dense layer,* because every unit is connected to all the other units of the other layer.

Deep neural networks have different types of layer connections. These differences are used to extract specific data. The most common layers are as follows:

- **Dense (fully connected):** In this type of layer, all the neurons of the previous layer are connected to the actual layer. This type of layer is useful for capturing general patterns in the data.

- **Convolutional:** In this type of layer, the number of neurons is reduced using a special reduction of the feature, which makes this type of layer optimal for grid-like data like images.

- **Recurrent:** In this type of layer, the output of the neuron is used as a weight input for the same node and as input for the next neuron. This type of layer is optimal when working with recursive structures such as text or other timed data.

- **Pooling:** In this type of layer, the information is reduced by executing a spatial dimensionality reduction. The goal is to retain only the essential information. This layer is used in combination with the convolutional layer in a convolutional neural network (CNN) architecture.

- **Dropout:** This type of layer is used to drop out some features to 0. The deep neural network essentially tries to find the coefficient to solve the input equation. In a simple world, any machine learning algorithm tries to define a mathematical function that can describe the data. Because you want to generalize the knowledge, the dropout layer will drop a set of data to avoid *overfitting* the function and then create a more generalized model.

Deep neural networks are powerful because they find the weight that makes the most accurate decision.

They do this using a process called *backpropagation.* In this technique, the error calculated for the iteration is sent back through the network. This adjusts the network's weight and then its data prediction.

Learning from the Data

At this point, it is important to clarify how a machine learning algorithm can learn from data. The perceptron formula was a very basic way to teach a machine to learn. You define a set of *features*, and when you receive input, you use the algorithm to see if the new set of features is positive or negative based on the threshold you defined.

This type of learning is not very feasible with different types of problems. The example of the perceptron can be used to determine if a person qualifies for a mortgage. But it's not good for generalizing a problem.

If you want to have a "thinkable" machine, you need to design an algorithm to generalize the data and adapt to the actual problem.

When you want to learn from the data, there are some components that allow you to do just that:

- You have an unknown target function. This can be for example an ideal formula for accepting/rejecting a mortgage.

- You have some training data. This is for example all the information about the actual mortgage delivered to the customer.

- You have a set of hypothetical formulas that you want to apply to learning.

- You have a learning algorithm.

All these components are mixed to define a final hypothesis about the possible learning algorithm.

The perceptron is a basic way to learn from some specific, well-defined data. But what happens when you want to learn from unseen data? To solve that problem, you need to use a probabilistic approach and reduce the error between the actual data calculated by the model and the training data.

The error calculated is used to adjust the weight for the input of the neuron. This adjusts the measure and results in a more descriptive formula. The most basic way to calculate the error is to subtract the predicted value from the input value.

The calculated error will be sent back to the function, and the weighted input will be subtracted and recalculated.

This way of calculating the error is not effective, but it gives you another important piece of information. When using algorithms for machine learning, you need to learn how to generalize the function. Because of the error, one iteration is not enough. This introduces the concept of an *epoch*.

An epoch is essentially the number of iterations you execute to have the algorithm *converge*. The convergence is essentially when the error between the predicted value and the input value is near 0.

The convergence in the algorithm is determined using a *learning rate*. The rate is applied to a *gradient descent*.

The learning rate is a factor applied to the function to adjust the weighted input. The gradient descent is essentially an optimization algorithm used to reduce the loss and error between two differentiable functions. In machine learning, this family of algorithms is used to manage the training rate and to have better generalization of the formula.

Gradient Descent

Gradient descent is a mathematical formula that's used to identify how much of the output change is based on a small change in the input. Figure 1-9 shows how a small learning rate can follow the curve better. However, how is the learning rate connected to the gradient descent?

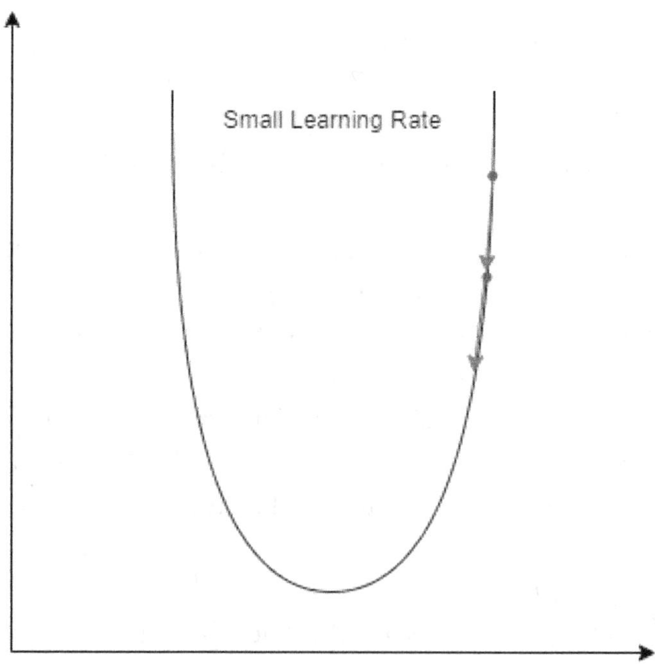

Figure 1-9. *An example of how the function follows the curve based on a small learning rate*

The learning rate is called a *hyperparameter*. A hyperparameter is a variable provided to the algorithm to regulate how to learn. It's used to improve the understanding of the underlying function in the data.

The adjustment made on the input parameters provides better output to the system. If the learning rate is too big, you can have something like Figure 1-10.

As you can see, the point learned from the function jumps from one side to another. You are not learning the real underlying function, but another one different from the original one.

The question now is how the learning rate connects to gradient descent. The gradient descent is defined as a mathematical algorithm. It determines how much the output changes with a small change in the input.

This is mainly because you can't just guess the learning rate and hope it's enough for learning the underlying function, because the function might never converge.

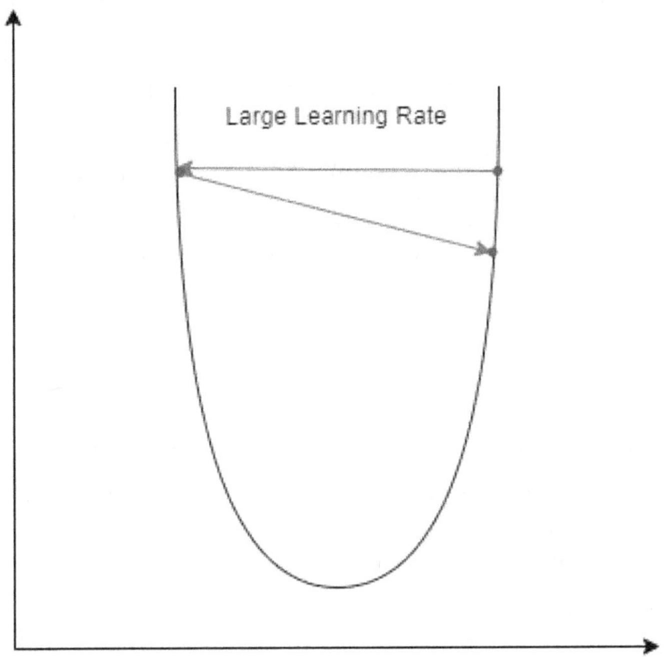

Figure 1-10. *The effect on the learning when you have a big learning rate*

To understand the needed input weight change and use backpropagation, you need an analytical method.

This example uses one of the different gradient descents. The basic type is a *batch gradient descent*. In this type of gradient descent, the adjustment is calculated after an *epoch*. An epoch is reached when the entire training set is passed through the model.

The error is calculated by subtracting the value of the predicted function from the input function. Then the descent is calculated based on the error and is backpropagated to the input. It is used to update the value of the weight.

This type of gradient descent is executed only once per epoch. This is not exactly optimal when dealing with deep learning. Another type of gradient descent is the *stochastic gradient descent*. In this case, the gradient descent is calculated using a single observation, not the entire training dataset. In this case, you send the first set of data from the training dataset.

In this case, you calculate the stochastic gradient descent and update the weight, then pass the new set of data using the updated weight.

The stochastic gradient descent is the preferred method with deep learning, because of the huge amount of data involved in the process of learning in a deep learning model. Stochastic gradient descent doesn't wait to finish the epoch. It uses a single set of features and data.

Up to now, the chapter has introduced the basics of machine learning and deep learning. It introduced the basics behind these two architectures, which allow machines to learn. It is now time to introduce the main topic, which is *generative artificial intelligence*.

Generative AI

Generative artificial intelligence (GenAI) is a type of deep learning. It uses probability to understand how to create data. There are four major families of generative models:

- Autoregressive generative models

- Flow-based generative models

- Latent variable generative models

- Energy-based generative models

Latent variable generative models can be split into two different sub-categories—implicit generative models and prescribed generative models. Examples of implicit generative models are generative adversarial networks (GANs). An example of a prescribed generative model is the variational autoencoder (VAEs).

Why is generative artificial intelligence becoming so important now? The answer is very simple. It is in line with the main goal of AI, which should not only be able to classify or predict a possible outcome but also to execute a task that requires human intelligence.

To better understand the importance of a deep generative model, this section explains a small example. Imagine for example you finish creating a classification model that's used for facial recognition to allow only authorized people to enter a business. Now suppose you train the neural network very well and give a classification of the person with a high probability $p(y|X)$. The model is quite a success and it's been used for some time, but one day you receive a call because some authorized people can't enter the building. What has changed? Maybe they look slightly different, which creates *noise* in the image. For example, a different beard or haircut. This noise is not interpreted by the normal classification algorithm simply because its job is to learn how to classify based on a specific set of data. It does not take into consideration any *uncertainty* in the data.

The algorithm for supervised or unsupervised learning classifies and identifies data based on the similarity of the data itself or based on the training data received in the input. A small change in the data can lead to a misclassification simply because the new set of data is less similar. This is why understanding generative deep learning becomes important.

To simulate human intelligence, the model for machine learning and deep learning needs to understand and incorporate any uncertainties connected to the data, and this involves a better understanding of the data as well.

Before continuing, I think is important to define human intelligence. The *Britannica* defines human intelligence as a "mental quality that consists of the abilities to learn from experience, adapt to new situations, understand and handle abstract concepts, and use knowledge to manipulate one's environment." Human intelligence involves different complex activities and the capacity to adapt to a new context. This capacity to learn and understand data becomes fundamental if we want to reach real artificial intelligence.

Understanding Uncertainty

Before you continue your journey into the deep generative model, I need to clarify why learning uncertainty and understanding the data matter. This is important when talking about decision-making.

To better understand why these concepts are so important, let's consider a simple example. This example is a basic classification algorithm. It needs to classify two classes: one green and one blue. Figure 1-11 shows a representation of the data. The first image on the left shows the data linearly separable.

A normal machine learning algorithm will learn that the blue region contains all the blue data, and the green region contains all the green data.

For classification, you can use two different approaches. The first approach is to define a classifier by modelling the conditional distribution $p(y|X)$.

In this type of modelling, the new data in the system, represented by an X on the right side of the image, is classified as blue.

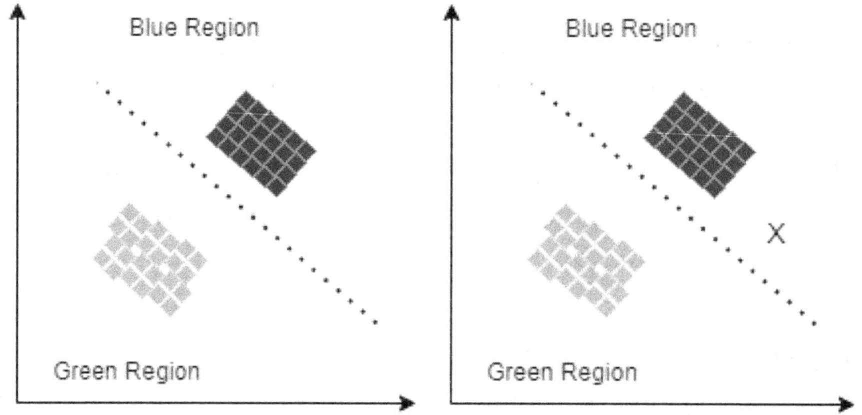

Figure 1-11. *A graphical representation of the data split into two regions*

The other approach you can follow is to classify the data using a joint distribution $p(X, y)$. You can compose the formula as per $p(X, y) = p(X)p(X)$.

In this type of distribution, you can see that the distribution $p(X)$ is far from the actual blue data, which means you can associate the X with the blue region because the marginal distribution of the data is far away from point X.

This simple example shows the importance of having an *understanding* of the environment first. You need to do this before trying to classify the data.

This is because the new data comes with a degree of *uncertainty*. If the algorithm can understand the data, it can identify and then remove the uncertainty.

From a *generative* point of view, knowing the distribution of $p(X)$ is essential for different reasons:

- It can tell if an object or data has been observed in the past or not.

- It can help properly weight the decision.

- It can be used to assess the uncertainty of the environment.

- It can be used to learn the interaction with the environment. For example, to identify all the objects with low $p(X)$.

- Because of the previous point, it can be used to generate new data; for example, identifying objects with high $p(X)$.

It's now obvious that for *generative modelling*, understanding the phenomena you represent is crucial. It's the key to generating new data.

Different Types of Generative Models

It should be clear now why you need deep generative models. Before exploring some of their applications, you need an understanding of the different types of models used to generate the data.

There are four major families of models that can be used to generate data:

- Autoregressive models

- Flow-based models

- Latent variable models

- Energy-based models

It's important to understand the difference between the models and how they each generate the new data.

Autoregressive Models: Learning from the Past

The first family of models for generating data is called *autoregressive modeling* (ARM). This family of models learns the data in an autoregressive manner.

In statistics, an autoregressive model predicts future data using past data. You can use this type of modelling to predict stock prices, for example. You look at the past value prices to predict future prices. Mathematically, this model is defined in this way:

$$p(X) = p(X_0) \prod_{i=1}^{D} p(x_i | X_{<i})$$

Where $X_{<i}$ indicates all the values of Xs up to the index i. The autoregression manner is used to calculate the conditional distribution of the data.

However, modelling all the conditional distributions for $p(x_i | X_{<i})$ can be highly inefficient from a computational point of view. You can reduce the inefficiency, at least when you generate audio or video, using a casual convolution. An example is present in Wavenet, a deep generative model for creating audio.

Autoregressive models are statistical models used to represent a random process. Autoregressive models work under the idea that past values can be used to predict the future. This idea assumes that past events influence the actual event.

This type of statistical technique is very popular for analyzing events that repeat over time. One example is stock market predictions.

Autoregressive models have three major processes:

- AR(0) is used for *white noise* and has no dependency between the terms, which means the previous value doesn't impact the actual one.

- AR(1) is where the current value is based on the immediately previous one.

- AR(2) is where the current value is based on the previous two values.

As you can see, the autoregressive model uses previous values to forecast the future. This is based on an assumption, which is that the fundamental forces that influenced the previous value have not changed over time.

Using an Autoregressive Model to Generate Data

An autoregressive model forecasts the possible output based on the values of the past, which is done because you model the conditional distribution of the data, and then the predicted value will become the new possible values.

Modelling the conditional distribution can be inefficient. This means you need to find a way to reduce the complexity.

The first attempt assumes *finite memory*. Because of that, you can assume that each variable depends on no more than two other variables. You can rewrite the formula in this way:

$$p(X) = p(x_1)p(x_2|x_1)\prod_{i=3}^{D}p(x_i|,x_{i-1}|,x_{i-2})$$

In this case, you limit the "memory" and then the computational complexity to just two previous variables. This limit makes it easier to solve the problem. But it has a downside. This type of model will use less memory, which can limit the complexity of the data you can represent.

For example, when looking at image or text, two variables are not enough. In this case, it's essential to have more memory to manage the complexity of the data.

Memory is a very important topic when considering generative deep learning. The capacity to "remember" previous data allows the model to create a more powerful and precise model. One of the fundamental improvements introduced in large language models (LLMs) is the capacity to maintain the entire sentence "in memory" before the model replies. This capacity enhances the level and makes this model more powerful than the normal NLP model.

Improving Memory Capacity: Long-Short-Term Memory

Autoregressive models have a drawback: they need complex computations. One solution is to implement a short-range memory. This reduces the number of variables used to forecast the value.

This type of model has a drawback. It's a problem with complex data, such as when image processing. To overcome this limitation, a new model is needed.

This model applies short-term memory to a recurrent neural network (RNN). This combination uses the power of the RNN with short-term memory, creating what's called *long short-term memory.*

Long short-term memory (LSTM) is an RNN that enables the model to expand its memory capacity to accommodate longer "memory".

An LSTM extends the RNN's capacity. In a typical RNN, we can only remember the past input. But, an LSTM lets the model memorize more than the previous output. This expands the capacity of the memory.

The LSTM adds specific mechanisms that allow the network to improve its "memory" capability:

- *The forgetting mechanism* forgets all the related information that is not worth remembering.

- *The saving mechanism* saves all the information that is important to remember.

The LSTM adds the concept of *gates*, which are used to define the LSTM capabilities and are important for enabling long-term memory capabilities:

- The *forget gate* is used to implement the forgetting mechanism. It is used to "forget" all the non-relevant information.

- *The learn gate* combines the current input, the event, with the short-term capability to understand if the actual information can be applied to the current input.

- *The remember gate* is where the "memory" takes place. In this gate, the information that's not forgotten and the actual event are combined. This creates a combination of information and events and allows the network to remember the data.

- *The use gate* makes the prediction. This is a combination of the other capabilities—long-term memory, short-term memory, and events— to make the prediction based on the "memory" of the past event.

Using the RNN, especially an LSTM, to enable the long range of memory helps improve the generative capacity, which is particularly important in text generation.

However, there is a downside to this technique. An RNN is essentially sequential. And because an LSTM comes directly from an RNN, it is also sequential.

This makes this type of architecture slow. There is another technique used to improve the long-range memory that doesn't use an RNN, but a CNN.

Improving Memory Using a Convolutional Network

Using a convolutional neural network (CNN) in the context of memory can be counterintuitive.

The papers published but Collober and Weston, "A Unified Architecture for Natural Language Processing: Deep Neural Networks with Multitask Learning," and Kalchbrenner, Grefenstette, and Blunsom, "A Convolutional Neural Network for Modeling Sentences," both show the capabilities of a convolutional neural network in this area.

I must clarify that this example uses a *casual one-dimensional convolution* because a normal one-dimensional convolution can be used for an autoregressive model.

Casual convolution is not dependent on future data. Executing the convolution is dependent on the kernel input k, which translates into a model that uses the previous value to predict the outcome. This makes this suitable for an autoregressive model.

This type of model is more suitable than a simple RNN to model sequential time-framed data. Examples of this architecture for generative modelling are WaveNet and PixelCNN.

This architecture has a price. While you can process the data in parallel when you sample a new object, you need to iterate through all the positions and iteratively predict all the probabilities and sample the new value. This means that because parameterized convolutions are used to parameterize the model, you must do the entire dataset D to get the final sample.

Flow-Based Model: The Complexity Behind the Simplicity

Flow-based models are another type of generative model. This model assumes that you can transform a simple distribution into a complex one. This change is done by implementing the *change of variables* theorem, essentially the theorem rebuilds the function of a known distribution, and the function must be *invertible*. This means that the model maps the function $x = f(z)$ to the function $z = f^{-1}(x)$.

An *invertible function* is a function that can be "reversed" to the original value. For example, if you have the function f and it takes the parameter a, which results in the value b, the inverse of f^{-1} must take the value b and result in a. This principle is used to create the new data. Essentially, this rebuilds the data based on the inversion of the original data.

You can express the conditional probability of the data $p(X)$ in this way:

$$p(X) = p\big(z = f(X)\big) J_{f(x)})$$

Where $J_{f(x)}$ is the Jacobian matrix and the f is parameterized using a deep neural networks. The neural networks must be able to calculate the Jacobian matrix. Examples of this architecture are NICE, RealNVP, or the most model Glow.

This model is attractive because of the tractability of the exact log-likelihood and the tractability of exact latent-variable inference—they support the parallelization of the task for training and synthesis.

Latent-Variable Models: Observing Reality to Find the Hidden Factor

Another type of model used to generate new data is the latent-variable model. It gained popularity after the publication of the paper by Goodfellow titled, "Generative Adversarial Networks".

The idea behind this model is based on the assumption that a lower-dimensional latent space corresponds to hidden factors in the data, and the conditional distribution $p(X|Z)$ can be used as a *generator*.

An example of a latent variable model is the *probabilistic principal component analysis*, which is for the linear model, the variational autoencoder, and the generative adversarial networks.

The idea behind the *latent variable models* is the introduction of latent variables z. The joint distribution is factorized this way:

$$p(X,Z) = p(Z)p(Z)$$

The latent variable z represents some factors in the data that allow the model to learn how to generate new data. To better understand this process, imagine that you want to generate an image of a dog.

When humans try to generate an image, they might first generate a silhouette of the dog, because this give us some basic information about the data we want to generate. Another factor to consider is the color of the fur. These factors are hidden characteristics that the latent-variable models try to understand and model with the latent variables.

The latent variable model, like the autoregressive, flow-based models, is a probabilistic model. It has the objective function of being the *log-likelihood function*. This function is closely related to the *Kullback-Leibler divergence* between the distribution of the data. These types of models are called *prescribed models*.

The Kullback-Leibler divergence is the statistical distance between two probabilities distributions. It's used to calculate the distance between the distribution. The shorter the distance, the more accurate the data that's generated.

A different approach is to calculate the *adversarial loss*. This type of approach is used for example in generative adversarial networks (GANs). The principle behind this type of network is to calculate the difference between the real data and the generated data using a *discriminator D(.)*. This discriminator uses the Dirac delta to calculate the distance and validate if the generated data is valid based on the input data. These are called *implicit models* because they calculate the distance between the data using some implicit value that's more difficult to identify.

Energy-Based Models: Using Physics to Generate New Data

Energy-based models are a new type of model based on the *canonical ensemble*. This is derived directly from statistical mechanics and represents the possible state of a mechanical system in thermal equilibrium. Because of their derivation, this model is referred to as *canonical ensemble learning* or *learning via canonical ensemble*.

If this model uses an energy function $E(x)$ to learn the distribution of the data and then create new data, the *Boltzmann machines* are a form of energy-based model and are used for the generative modelling. An energy-based model, or EBM, can be defined by this formula:

$$p(x) = \exp(-E(x))$$

Where $E(x)$ is the *energy function*. Because $exp(x)$ is always positive for all x values, this guarantees that there is no energy function. This will result in a probability of zero, and because you can choose any energy function, learning is easier.

The formula for the EBM is called the *Boltzmann distribution*, which is why energy-based models are called *Boltzmann machines.* There is no real guideline to when define a model is an energy-based model or a Boltzmann machine.

Discriminative vs. Generative

It's important to understand the difference between generative and discriminative modelling. Most problems addressed by machine learning are *discriminative* for nature. When we talk about a discriminative model, we talk about a model that is used to classify data.

From the point of view of probability, the discriminative model tries to model the *conditional probability* of x given y, and this can be expressed in this way: $p(y|x)$. On the other side, the generative modelling tries to model the *joint probability* of the x and y variables, and this can be express in this way: $p(x, y)$.

When we talk about discriminative modelling, we talk about a family of algorithms that work with labelled data or provide some sort of labelled data or group using a conditional probability. Imagine, for example, that you want to create a model to classify pictures. A discriminative model will learn the conditional probability—for example, it will learn that specific styles are connected to Picasso—and when the model receives new data, it will be able to classify the data based on the feature and the conditional probability that a specific feature is connected to a Picasso work.

On the other hand, *generative models* don't learn to classify the data, but they learn how the x and y observations are represented. The model doesn't label the data but essentially re-creates the same condition for the observation.

Imagine sending the same picture of Picasso to a generative model. In this case, the model doesn't learn how to classify the unseen data, but it tries to isolate and learn the features of x and y and determine how they are correlated. Learning this probability allows the generative model to re-create new data with a high probability of accuracy. This is an important difference and drives the development of generative artificial intelligence. I must note that some generative artificial intelligence models have discriminative functionalities. In particular, in GANs, the Discriminator part of the network uses a discriminative algorithm to classify if the data is part of the original data or not.

Conclusion

This chapter introduced the basics of AI. The chapter is essentially an introduction and did not go deeply into the math and the definitions of the different types of models.

The important message of this chapter is that generative artificial intelligence, or deep generative modelling, is not a magic tool that solves all problems. It's not a type of artificial intelligence similar to what we see in science fiction movies, but a simple implementation of normal probabilistic, statistical, and mathematical functions and theorems used to solve specific problems.

Generative AI is very important and will become more and more important. Artificial intelligence tries to produce tasks that require human intelligence. For this reason, you can't just rely on classification or regression models to emulate human intelligence. If you want to emulate human intelligence, you need to generate new data, which is where generative AI comes into play. Integrating generative AI with the other models of artificial intelligence can improve capacity and allow models to reach a general artificial intelligence.

## CHAPTER 2

Introduction to Julia

When developers want to develop a new artificial intelligence model, they must essentially write code that uses a lot of math. Julia is a general-purpose, open-source, dynamic, and high-performance language. It was developed by MIT in 2012.

Julia was made for use in science. That's why the majority of its use cases are connected to scientific computation and numerical analysis. This chapter explores the basics of Julia, which creates a foundation for completing the exercises in the following chapters.

The Reason Behind Julia

If you learn about how Julia was created, you can see a story of necessity. An article from *Wired* magazine explains the motivation behind Julia's development. MIT wanted a language that could be used to solve specific technical computing problems.

Stefan Karpinski is one of Julia's designers. He wrote software for a network simulator. To write the code, Karpinski needed to glue different languages together to suit the job. He asked for advice from Viral B. Shah, and he introduced him to Jeff Bezanson.

Bezanson believed that they could avoid the trade-off between the different languages. To design the language, they involved Alan Edelman, who was primarily a mathematician.

From their collaboration, Julia was created. The idea behind Julia is to have a simple language like Python that runs like C. In some cases, Julia has a performance similar to C.

Julia has a sophisticated compiler, which allows distributed parallel execution and high numerical accuracy.

In addition, an extensive mathematical function library makes Julia the perfect language for designing and developing scientific code.

© Pierluigi Riti 2026
P. Riti, *Introduction to Generative AI with Julia and Python*, https://doi.org/10.1007/979-8-8688-2329-9_2

Julia was presented to the world in September 2012, when the paper, "Julia: A Fast Dynamic Language for Technical Computing," was published.[1] In the paper, the authors describe the "why" behind Julia. The reason is because the usage of dynamic languages, like Python and R. These languages are popular in scientific computing. They are considered highly productive, but lack in performance.

Julia was designed to use modern techniques for running dynamic languages. The architecture of the language gives Julia the performance of a statically compiled language, like C. But, it also gives Julia the advantage of a dynamic language like Python. For example, it provides interactive behavior and productivity

Julia is an open-source language by nature, which attracted a lot of software developers. They create a set of modules and libraries that enrich the language.

Core Languages Feature

Julia was designed with some specific features and an eye on optimization. The core language is designed using these main components:

- The syntax layer translates the surface syntax into a suitable intermediate representation (IR).

- The symbolic language and corresponding data structure represent certain kinds of types and implementations of lattice operators for the previous type.

- Implementation of generic functions and dynamic multiple dispatch based on the previous type.

- Compiler-intrinsic functions for accessing the object model.

- Compiler-intrinsic functions for native arithmetic, bit string operations, and calling native functions.

- Mechanism for binding top-level names.

The syntax layer describes the function's body as a sequence of assignment operations, function calls, labels, and conditional branches.

The statements are executed in order, with function arguments evaluated eagerly, and passing all the values by reference.

At the core of Julia performance is the use of the JIT, just-in-time compilation, and the low level virtual machine (LLVM) compiler framework. The use of the LLVM allowed the designer to reach the performance of C, with the dynamism of Ruby.

Installing Julia

Installing Julia is easy. Go to `https://julialang.org/downloads/` and select the package for your operating system. Then, follow the instructions to install Julia on your local machine.

This book uses Google Colab. Not everyone can have enough power to run machine learning or deep learning algorithms. Google Colab offers a simple and cost-effective way to execute and run the model that's explored in the rest of the book.

An efficient way to test the code is to use `repl.it`. This site offers the capability to run basic Julia commands in a file or from the command line. I use it in the chapter, and before moving to the Colab, you must have a screen like that shown in Figure 2-1.

Figure 2-1. *The repl.it site with Julia console*

As you can see, this environment allows you to execute Julia in a cloud similar to a computer setup.

Command-Line Iteration with Julia

With Julia installed, or with the `repl.it` configured, you can now start to interact with the system without an editor.

The only command you need to execute is `julia`, which you do from the command line. This opens the Julia environment, as shown in Figure 2-2.

```
The latest version of Julia in the `release` channel is 1.10.2+0.x64.w64.mingw32. You currently have `1.10.0+0.x64.w64.m
ingw32` installed. Run:

  juliaup update

in your terminal shell to install Julia 1.10.2+0.x64.w64.mingw32 and update the `release` channel to that version.

               _
   _       _ _(_)_     |  Documentation: https://docs.julialang.org
  (_)     | (_) (_)    |
   _ _   _| |_  __ _   |  Type "?" for help, "]?" for Pkg help.
  | | | | | | |/ _` |  |
  | | |_| | | | (_| |  |  Version 1.10.0 (2023-12-25)
 _/ |\__'_|_|_|\__'_|  |  Official https://julialang.org/ release
|__/                   |

julia>
```

Figure 2-2. *The Julia REPL*

Julia, like other dynamic languages, has a *REPL*, which stands for *Read Evaluate Print Loop.* This environment let you do the first test with Julia. The best way to learn is to try.

Using REPL allows you to experiment quickly with the code, without using an editor. For example, you can use Visual Studio code if you use Windows. Let's now look at the basic components of the language using REPL.

You can use REPL to start basic experiments. Every time I start learning a new language, I try to print "Hello World" and Julia is no different. In the REPL, write the following:

```
println("Hello World")
```

This will print similar output:

```
julia> println("Hello World")
Hello World
```

The REPL will evaluate the command and produce the output. Consider another simple example, a sum of two numbers. In the REPL, write 2+2. The result will be similar to this:

```
julia> 2+2
4

julia>
```

In this case, Julia simply executes the operation and gives the result. REPL is useful for executing basic code tests.

Every program is made with some basic common structure: *variables, types, operators, data structure, control flows,* and *loops.* The following sections explain how Julia allows you to create this structure and build a complete program.

Variables

Variables in Julia work like every other language. They can be defined by a name and can be referred to during code execution.

In Julia, the variables are *case-sensitive,* which means a variable called `test` is different from a variable called `Test`.

The name must use Unicode UTF-8 characters. Because Julia is a scientific language, it is possible to use the Latex characters syntax to define a variable. In this case, to write the variable, you need to press the Tab to allow the compiler to write the variable. The rules for writing variables in Julia are simple:

- The variable name must start with a letter, uppercase or lowercase, an underscore _, or a Unicode code point.

- The other characters can include symbols, characters, and Unicode code points.

Let's see in practice how you can define some simple variables in Julia. You can use the REPL for testing:

```
julia> # Let's create a Latex variable, the alpha character, To do that
let's write \alpa

julia> \alpha
```

After writing \alpha in the command line, press Tab, and the result will be as follows:

```
julia> α
```

This will define a variable α. Now you can associate it with a value. For example, the number 1:

```
julia> α = 1
1

julia> α
1
```

The variable α is associated with the value 1. You can simply recall the variable and write the name of the variable.

Let's define some other variables using the rule defined before for Julia:

```
julia> _first_ = 10
10

julia> _First_ = 11
11

julia> test = 12
12
julia> Test = 3
3

julia> test =3/5
0.6

julia> test =3.5
3.5

julia> TesT=4
4
```

This example shows how easy it is to create a variable in Julia. The naming conventions for the variable in Julia are also simple.

The variable must start with an uppercase or lowercase letter and any words must be divided by underscores, such as `circle_radius`.

Variables don't help us write a complex program. Let's analyze the other components of the Julia language, starting with the operators.

Variable Types

At the core of any program, there is a set of variables used to represent specific types of data. Likewise, Julia has three basic data types:

- Numeric
- Float
- Strings

These basic data types are used to build the basics of the program.

Numeric Types

The numeric primitive data types represent the number in the code. These are the building blocks for all the arithmetic and computation operations.

The numeric types are numbers of objects in memory. The basic numeric types of Julia can be divided into:

- Integer
- Floating point

Integer data types can be split into other two subtypes—*signed* and *unsigned*. In addition to that are `char` and `boolean`. Table 2-1 recaps of all Julia's numeric data types.

Table 2-1. *The Numeric Types in Julia*

Name	Type	Size
Int8	Signed 8-bit	-2^7 to 2^7-1
UInt8	Unsigned 8-bit	0 to 2^7-1
Int16	Signed 16-bit	-2^15 to 2^15-1
UInt16	Unsigned 16-bit	0 to 2^15-1
Int32	Signed 32-bit	-2^31 to 2^31-1
UInt32	Unsigned 32-bit	0 to 2^31-1
Int64	Signed 64-bit	-2^63 to 2^63-1
UInt64	Unsigned 64-bit	0 to 2^63-1
Int128	Signed 128-bit	-2^127 to 2^127-1
UInt182	Unsigned 128-bit	0 to 2^127-1
Bool	True or False	1 or 0
Char	A 32-bit numeric type representing a Unicode character	
Float32	IEEE 754 32-bit floating-point	
Float64	IEEE 754 64-bit floating point	

By default, if you define numeric types in Julia without defining the size—for example, Int64 and Int32—Julia will use the size of the specific operating system architecture.

Julia has an internal variable to show the architecture types of the computer; it is possible to do that with the Sys.WORD_SIZE command.

```
julia> Sys.WORD_SIZE
64
```

It is also possible to check the minimum and maximum value for every numeric type with the typemin() and typemax() functions:

```
julia> typemin(Int32)
-2147483648
```

```
julia> typemax(Int32)
2147483647
```

As mentioned, Char is another numeric type. The difference between Char and the other numeric types is that Char represents a Unicode character. You can see the difference if you use the typemin() and typemax() functions:

```
julia> typemin(Char)
'\0': ASCII/Unicode U+0000 (category Cc: Other, control)
```

```
julia> typemax(Char)
'\xff\xff\xff\xff': Malformed UTF-8 (category Ma: Malformed, bad data)
```

In Julia, you don't need to explicitly define the type of a variable when you create a new one. But, you can always see the type using the typeof() function. You can open Julia's REPL and see this behavior at work:

```
julia> ex_ = 1
1
```

```
julia> ch = 'a'
'a': ASCII/Unicode U+0061 (category Ll: Letter, lowercase)
```

```
julia> typeof(ex_)
Int64
```

```
julia> typeof(ch)
Char
```

You can define a char when you create the variable using single quotes (').
For example, ch='a'. You can create a string using double quotes; for
example, st="a".

It's always possible to declare a specific type using a specific constructor. It is possible to create a Bool with the syntax b = Bool(0), which creates a Boolean with the value false:

```
julia> b = Bool(0)
false
```

Similarly, you can define other numeric types:

```
julia> in8=Int8(8)
8

julia> in16=Int16(16)
16

julia> typeof(in8)
Int8

julia> typeof(in16)
Int16
```

Another important type of numeric data is the floating type. The floating point number is a number with decimal point precision. Consider these examples:

```
julia> fl = 11.01
11.01

julia> typeof(fl)
Float64
```

String Data Type

A string is a finite sequence of characters. Julia supports the full Unicode characters using the UTF-8 encoding standard.

It is important to highlight some high-level features of the String data type in Julia:

- String is immutable, which means that every time you create a string, you create a new one.

- String is not a concrete type but an abstraction, which means that you can have different implementations of the String interface and all of them can be used transparently.

- Julia, like C and Java, represents the character Char with a first-class type; we see the Char in the numeric type because a character is a special 32-bit type Integer.

- Julia supports the full range of Unicode characters. Literal strings are always ASCII via the UTF-8 encoding, and it is possible to use a `transcode` function to convert to and from different Unicode encodings.

If you want to define a basic variable and initialize it as a string, you just need to use double quotes:

```
julia> str = "Hello, World."
"Hello, World."
```

`String` in Julia is conceptually a *partial function* from indices to characters. This means that you can use a specific index to access the specific character of the string.

Let's use the variable `str` to see how to access a specific character:

```
julia> str[2]
'e': ASCII/Unicode U+0065 (category Ll: Letter, lowercase)
```

Julia returned the character with the description of the type, the Unicode value, and the category. Let's see another character—in this case the character in position 6:

```
julia> str[6]
',': ASCII/Unicode U+002C (category Po: Punctuation, other)
```

As you can see, Julia returns the comma character. In addition, all the information connected to the Unicode is returned by Julia.

The information returned by Julia when you select a character from a string is essentially the Unicode information, including the type of character, the Unicode value, and the category. This information is returned in particular when you use the REPL and is mainly information about the type of variable.

In adding the its specific position, it is possible to read the position starting from the *end* of the string. It is possible to select a range of characters from the string itself.

The word end can be used as an index for a string. For example, if you want to select the last character from the previous string, you can use this syntax:

```
julia> str[end]
'.': ASCII/Unicode U+002E (category Po: Punctuation, other)
```

The last character of the string is returned. It is possible to apply some basic operator to the indicator end to select a different character. You can select the character at the end-3 position with this command:

```
julia> str[end-3]
'r': ASCII/Unicode U+0072 (category Ll: Letter, lowercase)
```

You can also get a substring from the original string using the colon (:) syntax. You can get the character starting from position 2 to position 5 in this way:

```
julia> str[2:5]
"ello"
```

The substring syntax will not return a character, but another string object. For example, you can select a single character using the substring syntax:

```
julia> str[6:6]
","
```

As you can see, the character is returned using double quotes, not single quotes. Let make the example clear. You can use the two syntaxes to see how typeof() will change:

```
julia> ch=str[6]
',': ASCII/Unicode U+002C (category Po: Punctuation, other)
julia> typeof(ch)
Char
```

The direct indexing of the value of the string returns a character, which you can see from the typeof(). Let's see how the same selection changes using the substring syntax:

```
julia> chr=str[6:6]
","

julia> typeof(chr)
String
```

In this case, the code returns a string. It is important to understand this mechanism if you want to take into consideration the memory consumption of the program you will write.

String Concatenation and Interpolation

Concatenation is one of the most common operations executed on a string; it's essentially the junction of two strings into one:

```
julia> first = "Hello"
"Hello"

julia> second="World"
"World"

julia> string(first, ", ", second)
"Hello, World"
```

This example is quite simple. It creates the first string and the second string and then creates a new string with the String constructor. The third string is created by adding the element of the other two strings.

This creates a new string with all the concatenated elements together. Julia has another operator that you can use to concatenate the string. The * operator :

```
julia> third = first * "," * second
"Hello,World"
```

The ^ operator concatenates the string for the number of times indicated by the right number. For example, if you want to repeat the same string five times, you can use syntax like this:

```
julia> four = first ^ 5
"HelloHelloHelloHelloHello"
```

Julia, like other languages, can *interpolate* the string. Similar to Perl, the $ operator is used to interpolate a string in Julia:

```
julia> first = "Hello"
"Hello"

julia> second = "World"
"World"

julia> greetings ="$first , $second"
"Hello , World"
```

This syntax is easier to read and follow. It is useful when you write your program because you can combine the string with some variable elaborated by the program itself.

Triple-Quoted String

The triple-quoted syntax is useful when you want to create multiline strings. For example, you can create strings like this:

```
julia> str="""
        Hello,
        World.
      """

"    Hello,\n    World.\n"
```

The triple-quoted string is useful when you want to comment on your code. You can remove the newline using the \ after the first string. For example, you can rewrite the string like so:

```
julia> str="""
        Hello,\
        World.
      """

"    Hello,World.\n"
```

In this case, the result is a string in just one line. In the triple-line, it is possible to use the " character without escaping. This produces a more complex string.

Operators

Julia operators are similar to Python and R operators and can be split into five families:

- Arithmetic

- Boolean

- Bitwise

- Updating

- Vectorized operators

This section briefly describes the operators in more detail. The first operator is the *arithmetic operator,* which can be split into two families:

- Unary operator
- Binary operator

Unary operators apply the operation to the same variable. Examples of unary operators are += and -=. Usage examples include:

```
julia> un_plus = 0
0
julia> un_plus +=2
2
julia> un_plus -=2
0
```

Note that the unary operator executes the operation, for example adding a value to the specific variable. Because of that, the variable must be defined and initiated. In other cases, you can have an undefined error.

Because of the mathematical nature of Julia, it contains some operators that are not present in other languages. Table 2-2 recaps all the mathematical operators.

Table 2-2. *Mathematical Operators in Julia*

Operator	Name	Description
+	Binary plus	Performs an addition
-	Binary minus	Performs a subtraction
*	Binary times	Performs a multiplication
/	Binary divide	Performs a division, x/y
÷	Binary integer divide	Performs a division x/y, truncates on the integer
\	Binary inverse divide	Performs an inverse division y/x
^	Binary power	Elevates the variable on the left to the value on the right
%	Binary reminder	Gives the remainder of the division

Julia follows the classic mathematical rules when you apply operators to a number. This means if you write something 3(2=3) between the 2 and the parenthesis, Julia sees multiplication.

The integer divide operator can be written in Julia by using \div and pressing Tab in the Julia REPL.

The Boolean operator works like every other language. Julia has five Boolean operators (see Table 2-3).

Table 2-3. *The Boolean Operator in Julia*

Operator	Name	Description
!	Negation	Indicate a negation of the value. For example, `true` becomes `false`.
&&	Short-circuiting AND	This is a short-circuiting AND. A short-circuiting doesn't evaluate the left operator if the right is negative.
||	Short-circuiting OR	This is a short-circuiting OR. A short-circuiting doesn't evaluate the left operator if the right is negative.
&	AND	This is the normal AND condition, which means the code evaluates both sides before deciding the result.
|	OR	This is the normal OR condition, which means the code evaluates both sides before deciding the result.

The other family of operator is the *bitwise* operator, listed in Table 2-4. This type of operator works directly on the bit mask of the value. They can be applied to any numerical value, similarly to the other operators.

Table 2-4. *The Bitwise Operator in Julia*

Operator	Name	Description
~x	Bitwise NOT	Executes the NOT operation to the variable x at a bit-level.
X & Y	Bitwise AND	Executes the AND operation at a bit level.
X | Y	Bitwise OR	Executes the OR operation at a bit level.
⊻	Bitwise XOR	Executes the XOR operation at a bit level.
⊼	Bitwise NAND (not AND)	Bitwises the NAND operation at a bit level.
⊽	Bitwise NOR (not OR)	Bitwises a NOT OR operation at a bit level.
>>>	Logical shift right	Shift the bit logically to the right.
>>	Arithmetic shift right	Shifts the bit arithmetically to the right.
<<<	Logical shift left	Shifts the bit logically to the left.
<<	Arithmetic shift left	Shifts the bit arithmetically to the left.

In Julia, it is possible to write XOR, NAND, NOR using the \xor <tab>, \nand <tab>, or \nor <tab> syntax, respectively.

The *updating operator* is a unary operator. This type of operator is essentially a binary, arithmetic, and bitwise operator; it updates the value of the variable with the value on the right. An update operator is created by placing an = immediately after the operator.

The updating operator can be created by adding the = sign to all the actual operators. For example, you can create the updating arithmetic operators using this simple syntax:

- +=

- /=

- -=

The last family of operators is the *vectorized operator*. This type of operator can be called a "dot" operator and can be applied to the binary operator.

This includes the + and ^ operators. These types of operators have the corresponding "dot" operator, such as .+ and .^.

This type of operator is designed to be applied to an array of elements by elements. For example, you can apply a .* 3 to an array and essentially multiply every element of the array by three. Listing 2-1 shows an example of using a "dot" operator in practice.

Listing 2-1. An Example of a "Dot" Operator

```
julia> arr=[2,3,4]
3-element Vector{Int64}:
 2
 3
 4

julia> arr.* 3
3-element Vector{Int64}:
  6
  9
 12
```

This code shows how a "dot" operator works. The operation is essentially applied to every single element of the array, and this type of operator is very useful when you need to execute an operation on an array.

Functions

Functions are building blocks for every language and are used to create logical units that solve a problem or a small part of it.

In Julia, a function is an object that maps a tuple of argument values and returns a value. In Julia, a function is not a pure mathematical function, which means that the function can be affected by the global state of the program. A function in Julia can be created using this basic syntax:

```
function <name of the function>(<value_1>,<value_2>,....<value_n>)
    <body of the function>
end
```

It is important to notice that Julia doesn't need any indentation. This is different from Python, and you use the word end to indicate the end of the function. You can create a basic function for the sum of two numbers in this way:

```
julia> function sum(num_1, num_2)
           num_1+num_2
       end

sum (generic function with 1 method)
```

This function has two arguments. The return is assigned by the last expression evaluated in the body of the function, in this case, the sum x+y.

Simple functions like this can be written in a more compact form in just one line, for example:

```
julia> sum(x,y)=x+y
sum (generic function with 1 method)
```

This type of function is defined as an *assignment form*, and it's common in Julia. This can be used only when you have a single assignment in the function.

Like every other language, a function can be called by using the name and passing the parameters into parentheses. For example, say you want to call the sum function defined previously:

```
julia> sum(2,3)
5
```

Because the function is an object in Julia, you can associate the actual function to a variable. The new variable becomes a function with the same body, for example:

```
julia> new_sum = sum
sum (generic function with 1 method)

julia> new_sum(3,3)
6
```

As you can see, new_sum becomes a function sum and you can use it to execute the same operation of the sum.

In Julia, the argument is *passed by reference*, which means that the values are not copied but are passed to the functions. This means that when you change the value of the variable in the function, you change the value of the caller variable as well. Let's look at this behavior with a short code example:

```julia
julia> arr = [10,15]
2-element Vector{Int64}:
 10
 15

julia> b = 10
10

julia> function test(x,y)
          x[1] = 12
          y = 5 + y
          return y
       end
test (generic function with 1 method)

julia> test(arr, b)
15

julia> arr
2-element Vector{Int64}:
 12
 15

julia> b
10
```

As you can see in the code, you first define an array called arr and b, and you associate the value with the variable.

The test(x,y), function defines a new value for the arr array in position 1 in the body. The b variable has a new binding associated with the variable y, which avoids changing the value of the variable passed by reference to the function.

For example, if you see the value of the arr variable passed to the function, you can see the new value associated with position 1.

Julia uses a common convention to indicate a function that has one of its arguments mutated. This is indicated by adding an exclamation mark (!) after the name of the function. For example, the previous function `test(x,y)` becomes `test!(x,y)`.

In the previous example, you see the use of the keyword `return`. By default this is the last expression evaluated in the body of the function. `return` can be used to terminate the function early.

As in many languages, a function can return a specific type, similar to what is done for using the syntax `::<type of value>`. For example, you can define a function that can return an integer:

```julia
julia> function ret_value(x,y)::Int32
           return x +y
       end
```

In this case, the function will return an `Int32` type. In Julia returning a value is very rare, because it's preferred to not define a type, to avoid overflow issues, and leaves Julia to infer and return the type.

In Julia, if you want to return a `void` function, you can use the `nothing` keyword. This is more a convention for making sure a function doesn't return any value. The syntax in this case is similar to this:

```julia
julia> function void_fun(x, y)
           x+y
           return nothing
       end
void_fun (generic function with 1 method)

julia> void_fun(2,3)

julia>
```

As you can see, the `void_fun(x,y)` function has a body with no return. This is shown when you call the function and you don't see the value in return.

Anonymous Functions

In Julia, the functions are first-class objects. They can be assigned to a variable, and they can be called using the standard call syntax for the function. They can be used as arguments and can be returned as values. A function can also be created anonymously. An anonymous function is a function without a name and can be created using:

- What is similar to a lambda definition

- A function without a name

An anonymous function created using a lambda syntax is similar to this:

```
julia> an=x -> 10x + 5
```

```
julia> an(5)
55
```

This creates an anonymous function and associates the function with the an variable. You can use the function simply by calling an(5), which will execute the lambda function and return the calculated value.

The other way to define an anonymous function is to create the function without a name and associate the function with a variable:

```
julia> an2=function(x)
          x^2+2x-1
       end
```

```
julia> an2(10)
119
```

The anonymous function is not intended to be used with a variable, but to be used as an argument for a function. A classic example is a map, which applies a function to each element of an array:

```
julia> map(x -> 10x +2x + 5, [1,5,-2])
3-element Vector{Int64}:
  17
  65
 -19
```

This is a perfect example of an anonymous function used in a map. The anonymous function is applied to any element of the array. Anonymous functions can have more than one argument; the syntax is similar to `(x,m,b) -> mx+b`. An example is similar to this:

```julia
julia> ((x,b)-> 2x+b)(2,3)
7
```

Define the Argument Type

In Julia, you don't need to define the type of variables. However, in some occasions defining them can be useful. In a function you can specify the type of the argument by appending `::<Type Name>` after the argument name. For example, you could create a function where you define a specific type of variable:

```julia
julia> function sum(a::Integer, b::Integer)
            a+b
        end
```

Specifying the type of argument in a function normally doesn't have an impact on the performance, but sometimes you might choose to define the type of argument in the function:

- *Dispatch*, where you define the different types of variables that can allow you to create different types of functions. For example, you can define another function called `sum` but with the parameter as a Float. The function will look like `sum(a::Float32, b::Float32) = a+b`. In this way, you can use the float number to have the `sum` value.

- *Correctness*, where you define the type of value and make sure the value returns a certain type of value.

A problem with a defined type argument is the overflow. For example, if you define a function with two integer type numbers and the sum of the number goes over the definition of the type defined—for example, a 16-bit or a 32-bit value—the program can return an overflow.

Control Flow

Control flow is the bread and butter of every program. This is essentially the order in which the computer executes statements in a script. In Julia, there are several types of control flow constructs:

- Compound expressions

- Conditional evaluation

- Repeated evaluations (loops)

The first five control flows are standard for every high-level programming language, and the last one is for *tasks* that are specific for Julia. They provide a non-local control flow, making it possible to switch between temporarily suspended computations.

Compound Expressions

Compound expressions are used to compress several sub-expressions in one simple structure. The result is essentially a variable created using some kind of logic. In Julia you can create a compound expression in two ways:

- Using the `begin...end` syntax

- Using the `;` syntax

The `begin..end` syntax is created like this:

```
z = begin
          x=1
          y=2
          if x <1
              x + y
          else
              x * y
          end
          end
```

The z variable in this case is determined by the value of the value of x and y. Of course, the x and y variables can be defined outside the `begin..end` syntax.

Compound expressions are very simple and because of that they can be written in a single line using the ; syntax:

```
julia> z =(x=2; y=5; if x>2 x*y else x+y end)
7
```

You can of course include the x and y variables outside the definition and, because of that, change the value of z. The compound expression introduces another control flow, probably one of the most commonly used—the conditional evaluation.

Conditional Evaluation

A conditional evaluation evaluates a condition and executes a piece of code based on the condition. The anatomy of a conditional evaluation is if-elseif-else. An example of conditional evaluation is as follows:

```
julia> if x < y
           println("Y is bigger")
       elseif x > y
           println("X is bigger")
       else
           println("X and Y are equal")
       end
```

In Julia, the conditional evaluation is closed with an end. As with every other language, the elseif and else are optional. The if-elseif-else expression is evaluated until one of the one conditions is true. When the first condition reaches the condition, it is executed.

In Julia, it is possible to use what is called a *ternary operator,* which is created with the ?: syntax. It is used when a conditional choice between single expression values is required. Here's an example:

```
julia> a =1; c=3
3

julia> println(x < y ? "Less" : "Bigger")
Bigger
```

Repeated Evaluations (Loops)

Julia has two constructors for repeated evaluations:

- `while`

- `for`

The `while` and `for` loops are similar in usage; the difference between the two is essentially the condition for executing the loop. An example of the `while` loop is as follows:

```julia
julia> i = 1
1

julia> while i <= 5
           println(i)
           global i +=1
       end
1
2
3
4
5
```

The `while` loop evaluates the i <=5 condition. If the variable i is more than five, the loop will not be executed.

The `global i +=1` code is used to change the global variable i. In Julia, the scope of variables is local. If you want to change a variable external to the scope of the code, for example outside the `while` loop, you need to add the `global` keyword before the variable name.

The `for` loop, on the other hand, counts up and down a variable, which makes it easier to read. An example of a `for` loop is as follows:

```julia
julia> for i=1:5
           println(i)
       end
```

```
1
2
3
4
5
```

This `for` loop is the same as the `while` loop, but the syntax is easier to read and the code count is based on a range of values.

The `for` loop can be used to iterate over any container. In this case, you can use the `in` keyword, as follows:

```julia
julia> for i in ["foo", "bar", "baz"]
           println(i)
       end
foo
bar
baz
```

Sometimes it is necessary to break the execution of the loop. In this case, you can use the `break` keyword to interrupt the loop. Here's an example:

```julia
julia> for i=1:100
           println(i)
           if i >= 10
               break
           end
       end
1
2
3
4
5
6
7
8
9
10
```

In this case, the execution will be stopped when the loop reaches the tenth iteration exit from the loop. The equivalent of the while loop is as follows:

```julia
julia> while true
           i += 1
           println(i)
           if i>=10
               break
           end
       end
1
2
3
4
5
6
7
8
9
10
```

---

while true executes an infinite loop. In this case, it is important to have a break condition or the loop will never be finished.

There are also some cases when you'll want to skip a step in the loop. In this case, you can use the continue keyword to skip a specific step. The syntax is as follows:

```julia
julia> for i=1:20
           if i % 3 != 0
               continue
           end
           println(i)
       end
3
6
```

9
12
15
18

Collections in Julia

A *collection* is an essential data structure in any programming language. Julia has four types of collections:

- Arrays

- Tuples

- Dictionary

- Sets

The collection may be *indexable* or *associative*. An indexable collection is a collection where you can identify the elements of the collection using an index. Examples of indexable collections in Julia are arrays and tuples. In the case of Julia, the index of a collection starts with 1.

On the other hand, *associative* collections are collections where you don't have a specific index to access an element. Instead, you use a key. (In Julia, `Dict` is an associative collection.) Because of that, an associative collection is not indexable. In addition, a collection can be *mutable* or *immutable*. A mutable collection can be updated with a new element or by modifying an existing element. An immutable collection can't be modified. Mutable collections in Julia are arrays and dicts; immutable collections are tuples and sets.

In Julia, sets represent a special case of collection. This type of collection is immutable, non-indexable, and non-associative.

The next sections discuss the different types of collections in Julia. The first one, and probably the most commonly used, is the array.

Arrays in Julia

An *array* is an ordered collection of elements. In Julia, an array is defined using square brackets [ ]. An array can be created empty;—you just associate the variable name with the square—or one can be made with some initial value. An array can be created with any type on it, and different types can be present in the same array.

```julia
julia> empty_array = []
Any[]

julia> integer_array=[1,3,4,6]
4-element Vector{Int64}:
 1
 3
 4
 6

julia> mixed_array=[1,"hello",'a', 1.10]
4-element Vector{Any}:
 1
  "hello"
  'a': ASCII/Unicode U+0061 (category Ll: Letter, lowercase)
 1.1

julia>
```

As you can see from this example, Julia interferes with the elements of the array and determines what types of collections they are. In case of an empty array, the type will be Any(). This is the same type used for the mixed array, because the language doesn't know yet what type of data will be stored in the array. In Julia, an array can also contain functions:

```julia
julia> a =x -> x+5
#2 (generic function with 1 method)

julia> b =x -> x*5
#4 (generic function with 1 method)
```

```
julia> function_array=[a,b]
2-element Vector{Function}:
 #2 (generic function with 1 method)
 #4 (generic function with 1 method)
```

As mentioned, an array is an index collection, which means you can access an element of the collection simply using the index. If, for example, you wanted to access the second element of the array, you would use this syntax:

```
julia> integer_array[2]
3
```

It is also possible to read a range of elements from an array. In this case, what you have is another array with the element selected from the original one, like so:

```
julia> integer_array[2:3]
3-element Vector{Int64}:
 3
 4
```

Similarly to the selection, you can set the element of an array using the index of the element. For example, if you wanted to change the element in the first position of the integer_array, you would use this code:

```
julia> integer_array[1]=5
5
julia> integer_array
4-element Vector{Int64}:
 5
 3
 4
 6
```

One characteristic of arrays in Julia is the capacity to *unpack* the elements of the array into variables. Consider this example:

```
julia> first,second,third,fourth=integer_array
4-element Vector{Int64}:
 5
 3
```

```
  4
  6

julia> first
5
```

You can use the push! function to manipulate an array. You append an element at the end of an array. For example, to append an element to the empty array you created before, you would use this code:

```
julia> push!(empty_array,5)
1-element Vector{Any}:
  5
```

Another function you can use is pop!, which selects the last element from the array and removes it from the array:

```
julia> pop!(mixed_array)
1.1
```

If you want to combine two arrays, you can use the append! function, which appends the second array to the first one:

```
julia> append!(empty_array, mixed_array)
4-element Vector{Any}:
  5
  1
   "hello"
   'a': ASCII/Unicode U+0061 (category Ll: Letter, lowercase)
```

Vector is a special type of array. The syntax for creating a vector is the same as you use to create an array. The only difference is that you don't use the comma to separate the elements:

```
julia> row_vector=[5,4,6,7]
4-element Vector{Int64}:
  5
  4
  6
  7
```

You can create an n-dimensional vector simply by separating the elements of the vector with semicolons:

```
julia> multidim_vector=[2 3 4;4 5 6;7 9 1]
3×3 Matrix{Int64}:
 2  3  4
 4  5  6
 7  9  1
```

Tuples

Tuples are immutable collections, similar to arrays. The elements of a tuple can be all of the same types or can be mixed. The main difference between arrays and tuples is that the elements of the tuples can't be updated. The syntax for creating a tuple is to add the elements in parentheses ( ):

```
julia> tuple_elements=(10,'a',"big")
(10, 'a', "big")
```

Dictionaries

A *dictionary* is a key-value pair of arguments of the collection. They are created in Julia using the Dict function. They can be created in two ways:

- As an *untyped dictionary*, where the type of the value for the key and the value are not defined.

- As a *typed dictionary*, where the type of the value and the key are defined.

Take a look at the following examples for how to create a dictionary in Julia:

```
julia> typed_dictionary=Dict{Integer, String}(1=>"a", 2=>"b")
Dict{Integer, String} with 2 entries:
  2 => "b"
  1 => "a"
```

This code creates a typed dictionary. The key is an integer and the value is a string. If you want to create an untyped dictionary, you simply remove the type of the key and the value:

```
julia> untyped_dictionary=Dict(1=>"a", 2=>"b")
Dict{Int64, String} with 2 entries:
  2 => "b"
  1 => "a"
```

Access to a dictionary is made by the key. The syntax is as follows:

```
julia> untyped_dictionary[2]
"b"
```

To update the value of a dictionary, you access the element and update it with the new value:

```
julia> untyped_dictionary[2] = "c"
"c"

julia> untyped_dictionary
Dict{Int64, String} with 2 entries:
  2 => "c"
  1 => "a"
```

You can see all the keys of a dictionary using the keys() function, which will return a set with all the keys present in the dictionary:

```
julia> keys(untyped_dictionary)
KeySet for a Dict{Int64, String} with 2 entries. Keys:
  2
  1
```

You can check for the presence of a key in a dictionary using the haskey() function, as follows:

```
julia> haskey(untyped_dictionary, 3)
false

julia> haskey(untyped_dictionary, 1)
true
```

This function will return a Boolean value indicating whether the key is present in the dictionary.

Sets

Julia's sets are similar to arrays. The main difference is that sets are unordered collections of unique elements. This means that it is not possible to add the same element twice in a set. Set are created using the Set() keyword constructor. The syntax for creating a set is as follows:

```julia
julia> set_example=Set([1,2,3,1])
Set{Int64} with 3 elements:
  2
  3
  1
```

This example shows how the set can accept only one element of the type. When I create the set, I add two values 1, but because the set is unique, the last one is removed from the collection.

Elements in a set can be read by indexing a set because they are unordered and there is no fixed index. To read the element from a set, you need to use a for loop. For example, if you wanted to read the element in set_example, you could use code like this:

```julia
julia> for i in set_example
          println(i)
       end
2
3
1
```

If you want to add an element to a Set, you can use the push! function similarly to what was done with the array:

```julia
julia> push!(set_example,4)
Set{Integer} with 4 elements:
  4
  2
  3
  1
```

Working with Files in Julia

Open a file in Julia the same way you open it in Python: use the open(path) function. The function returns an object that represents the file. For example, you can open a file this way:

```
julia> file_example=open("C:/Julia_Example/Julia_Example.txt")
IOStream(<file C:/Julia_Example/Julia_Example.txt>)
```

Now you can see the open function and return an IOStream. The file_example variable becomes a *file handler*, but because it is a Stream, when you are done with the file, you need to close it with the close function, like so:

```
julia> close(file_example)
```

With the file handler open, you can start to do some basic operations on the file. To read the file you can use the readlines function, which returns an array of String where the elements of the array are the lines of the file separated by the newline character (\n):

```
julia> readlines(file_example)
2-element Vector{String}:
 "This is an example"
 "With more than one line"
```

It's possible to iterate the file with a for or while loop. You can, for example, read the contents of the file this way:

```
julia> file_example=open("C:/Julia_Example/Julia_Example.txt")
IOStream(<file C:/Julia_Example/Julia_Example.txt>)

julia> for line in readlines(file_example)
        println(line)
    end

This is an example
With more than one line
```

You can also use a more compact syntax to read a file line by line:

```julia
julia> open("C:/Julia_Example/Julia_Example.txt") do file
           while ! eof(file)
               s = readline(file)
               println("$s")
           end
       end
This is an example
With more than one line
```

This code essentially associates the object to the file handler and uses the function `eof(file handlers)` in a `while` loop to read the file. This type of syntax doesn't require you to close the file handler; it will automatically be closed when you exit from the loop.

To write a file, you need to change the way you create the file handler. You need to use the `w` parameter to make the file handler "writable." The file handler is created using the `write` function instead of the `readline` command:

```julia
julia> file=open("C:/Julia_Example/Julia_Example.txt","w")
IOStream(<file C:/Julia_Example/Julia_Example.txt>)

julia> write(file, "A new file in the file")
22

julia> close(file)
```

This code uses the `w` parameter, which means that Julia will cancel all the previous data from the file and change it with the newline. If you want to append the data to the file, you can use the `a` parameter, which will append the data to the end of the file.

Note   When you add an element to the file, you need to use the operating system's newline character if you want the element to be added as a new line. In the case of Linux/UNIX, you can use \n and in the case of Windows, you need to use \r\n.

Configuring Julia in Google Colab

Google Colab, or "colaboratory," is a browser editor used to execute Python code online. This environment is similar to Jupyter Notebook. In Colab you can execute the code in a cloud environment and have a GPU at your service. First, to start to work and install Julia in your Colab, you connect to the Google Colab itself. In a browser, navigate to Google Colab, `https://colab.research.google.com/`, which will connect you to a Google Colab notebook. Open a new notebook and add this code to the code section:

```
%%shell
set -e

#---------------------------------------------------#
JULIA_VERSION="1.10.3"
JULIA_PACKAGES="IJulia BenchmarkTools"
JULIA_PACKAGES_IF_GPU="CUDA" # or CuArrays for older Julia versions
JULIA_NUM_THREADS=2
#---------------------------------------------------#

if [ -z 'which julia' ]; then
# Install Julia
JULIA_VER='cut -d '.' -f -2 <<< "$JULIA_VERSION"'
echo "Installing Julia $JULIA_VERSION on the current Colab Runtime..."
BASE_URL="https://julialang-s3.julialang.org/bin/linux/x64"
URL="$BASE_URL/$JULIA_VER/julia-$JULIA_VERSION-linux-x86_64.tar.gz"
wget -nv $URL -O /tmp/julia.tar.gz # -nv means "not verbose"
tar -x -f /tmp/julia.tar.gz -C /usr/local --strip-components 1
rm /tmp/julia.tar.gz

# Install Packages
nvidia-smi -L &> /dev/null && export GPU=1 || export GPU=0
if [ $GPU -eq 1 ]; then
JULIA_PACKAGES="$JULIA_PACKAGES $JULIA_PACKAGES_IF_GPU"
fi
for PKG in 'echo $JULIA_PACKAGES'; do
echo "Installing Julia package $PKG..."
julia -e 'using Pkg; pkg"add '$PKG'; precompile;"' &> /dev/null
done
```

```
# Install kernel and rename it to "julia"
echo "Installing IJulia kernel..."
julia -e 'using IJulia; IJulia.installkernel("julia", env=Dict(
"JULIA_NUM_THREADS"=>"'"$JULIA_NUM_THREADS"'"))'
KERNEL_DIR='julia -e "using IJulia; print(IJulia.kerneldir())"'
KERNEL_NAME='ls -d "$KERNEL_DIR"/julia*'
mv -f $KERNEL_NAME "$KERNEL_DIR"/julia

echo ''
echo "Successfully installed 'julia -v'!"
echo "Please reload this page (press Ctrl+R, ⌘+R, or the F5 key) then"
echo "jump to the 'Checking the Installation' section."
fi
```

This will install Julia 1.10.3 on your Google Colab. The next step is to restart your runtime. To do that, execute the Runtime-->Restart Session command, which will change the runtime session from Python to Julia.

You can check the version of Julia by adding a new line under the previous code and the `versioninfo()` command. If the installation is correct, you will get an answer like this:

```
Julia Version 1.10.3
Commit 0b4590a5507 (2024-04-30 10:59 UTC)
Build Info:
  Official https://julialang.org/ release
Platform Info:
  OS: Linux (x86_64-linux-gnu)
  CPU: 2 × Intel(R) Xeon(R) CPU @ 2.20GHz
  WORD_SIZE: 64
  LIBM: libopenlibm
  LLVM: libLLVM-15.0.7 (ORCJIT, broadwell)
Threads: 2 default, 0 interactive, 1 GC (on 2 virtual cores)
Environment:
  LD_LIBRARY_PATH = /usr/local/nvidia/lib:/usr/local/nvidia/lib64
  JULIA_NUM_THREADS = 2
```

As you can see, Julia is installed and ready to be used. An important note to keep in mind is to check the runtime when you close and restart your Julia notebook. You can check the actual runtime using the Runtime➤Change Runtime menu command. This shows what type of runtime you are using. If it's Julia, you don't need to do anything. But if it's Python, you need to rerun the previous command and execute the instruction to reset the runtime.

With the runtime now installed and configured, you can write and execute Julia code in the Google Colab.

It is possible to find the complete Colab notebook with the Julia configuration on the GitHub connected with the book. When you write the code, I use this notebook to add the line of code needed to create the generative model. You don't need to run the Julia installation, but just the line you need to execute the code. You will see this in the rest of the book.

Managing the Package in Julia

Like any other language, Julia has a way of managing external packages. Knowing how to use the package manager is very important, because most of the functionality you will use in the book is from external packages. For example, if you want to work with CSV, you need to import the CSV.jl package. Or if you want to use Pandas, you need to import the Pandas.jl package. You can install a Pandas package in Julia this way:

```
julia> using Pkg
```

```
julia> Pkg.add("Pandas")
```

This will install the new package in Julia. When the package is installed in your environment, you can import and use it with the using keyword followed by the name of the package. For example, you can import and create a Pandas dataframe this way:

```
julia> using Pandas
```

```
julia> df = DataFrame(Dict(:age=>[27, 29, 27], :name=>["James", "Jill",
"Jake"]))
    age   name
0   27   James
```

```
1    29    Jill
2    27    Jake
```

This code creates a new Pandas dataframe with some basic data. In the following chapters, you'll import and use many different types of libraries and explore the use of the package manager in Julia.

Conclusion

This chapter introduced the Julia language. The goal of this chapter was to introduce the basics and explain Julia's functionality. However, compressing an entire language into one chapter is impossible and this chapter is just an introduction.

The goal of the book is to explain the Julia language in order to build deep generative models. The rest of the book explains, when needed, other Julia features, so that you can write and develop a fully deep generative model with Julia and improve your knowledge of the Julia language.

## CHAPTER 3

Introduction to Python

Python is undoubtedly one of the most commonly used languages for AI. This chapter introduces Python to non-Pythonists. Python is one of the languages used in this book, and this chapter introduces the basics of Python and prepares the ground for the rest of the book.

Python Overview

Python is an open-source, general-purpose, high-level language, released in 1991 by Guido Van Rossum. The name Python was chosen after the British comedy group Monty Python. The language's design philosophy is to emphasize readability. It does this using the indentation.

Python is a dynamically typed language. Another characteristic of the language is the use of a garbage collector. This means the language will remove unused objects from memory.

The philosophy behind the design of the feature was summarized in the "Zen of Python (PEP 20)". The language was designed to use indentation to end strings. This makes the language easy to read because the developer is forced to indent the code.

Another feature that makes Python more readable is the use of English keywords, whereas other languages use punctuation.

Like Julia, Python uses a REPL. It lets the developer quickly test the code and explore the language's functionality. Python is an easy-to-learn language and it has a very highly efficient high-level data structure.

The ecosystem created around Python makes the language very popular. At the time I wrote this book, Python was ranked number one. Because of its flexibility, Python can be used everywhere, from backend development to embedded development.

This chapter explains the language and shows how fun and easy it is to learn.

© Pierluigi Riti 2026
P. Riti, *Introduction to Generative AI with Julia and Python*, https://doi.org/10.1007/979-8-8688-2329-9_3

Using REPL in Python

If you have Python installed on your machine, you can access the REPL by typing python at the command line. This will open the REPL environment and you should see something similar to Figure 3-1.

```
Python 3.12.3 (tags/v3.12.3:f6650f9, Apr  9 2024, 14:05:25) [MSC v.1938 64 bit (AMD64)] on win32
Type "help", "copyright", "credits" or "license" for more information.
>>>
```

Figure 3-1. *The Python command line REPL*

Similarly to Julia, you can use the repl.it site. This helps you create a full Python environment. In this chapter, you can use the command line or repl.it to test your code.

The first taste of Python is the classic "Hello World" message. Open the command line or use the repl.it site and enter this command:

```
print("Hello World")
```

The result is shown in Figure 3-2.

```
~/IntroductionGenerativeAIPython$ python
Python 3.10.14 (main, Mar 19 2024, 21:46:16) [GCC 13.2.0] on linux
Type "help", "copyright", "credits" or "license" for more information.
>>> print("Hello World")
Hello World
>>> 
```

Figure 3-2. *The result of the "Hello World" print command*

To execute the Hello World command, I used the repl.it site; this is the preferred method in this chapter.

Before you continue to use and explore Python, you need some familiarity with the REPL environment.

REPL stands for *Read, Evaluate, Print, Loop*. You can input a command into it and get an immediate result in Python. In the REPL environment, you can use methods that help you understand the Python programs.

For example, the type() command returns the type of the object associated with the variable:

```
>>> string_variable = "test"
>>> type(string_variable)
<class 'str'>
>>>
```

Another useful command is dir(), which returns all the possible methods available for the variable.

If you use the dir() command on the string_variable variable, you will get a result like this:

```
>>> dir(string_variable)
['__add__', '__class__', '__contains__', '__delattr__', '__dir__',
'__doc__', '__eq__', '__format__', '__ge__', '__getattribute__',
'__getitem__', '__getnewargs__', '__gt__', '__hash__', '__init__',
'__init_subclass__', '__iter__', '__le__', '__len__', '__lt__', '__mod__',
'__mul__', '__ne__', '__new__', '__reduce__', '__reduce_ex__', '__repr__',
'__rmod__', '__rmul__', '__setattr__', '__sizeof__', '__str__',
'__subclasshook__', 'capitalize', 'casefold', 'center', 'count', 'encode',
'endswith', 'expandtabs', 'find', 'format', 'format_map', 'index',
'isalnum', 'isalpha', 'isascii', 'isdecimal', 'isdigit', 'isidentifier',
'islower', 'isnumeric', 'isprintable', 'isspace', 'istitle', 'isupper',
'join', 'ljust', 'lower', 'lstrip', 'maketrans', 'partition',
'removeprefix', 'removesuffix', 'replace', 'rfind', 'rindex', 'rjust',
'rpartition', 'rsplit', 'rstrip', 'split', 'splitlines', 'startswith',
'strip', 'swapcase', 'title', 'translate', 'upper', 'zfill']
>>>
```

These are the methods that you can apply to a string object. There are a lot of methods to remember, and many you won't use so often.

Luckily, there is a method for accessing these commands. The help() command returns information about a specific method. Let's test it:

```
>>> help(string_variable.upper)

Help on built-in function upper:
upper() method of builtins.str instance
    Return a copy of the string converted to uppercase.
(END)
```

When you use the `help()` command, Python opens a manual page for the command. To exit the page and come back to REPL, press the q button.

Indentation in Python

Python was made for clarity. It uses indentation to manage the end of a block of code. An example of Python code is shown in the following example:

```
>>> first=1
>>> if first:
...     second=2
...     if second:
...         print("Second block")
...     print("First block")
```

The code clearly shows how indentation works in Python. The indentation rules are simple. The line needs to be indented. This code starts with the `if first:` which needs to have four spaces or a Tab from the start of the previous line.

You can see the declaration of the `second=2` variable, and you can naturally follow the flow of the program. You can determine where the instruction starts to be nested and this improves the readability of the code itself.

There is one thing you need to remember. The indentation in Python determines the group of instructions. A wrong indentation can easily make the code consider the wrong variable assignment and this can change the way the code acts.

Basic Python Data Types

Indentation is an important part of the Python language. But if you want to write a fully functional program, you need to understand how to use the basic data types for the language.

As with other languages, Python defines some basic data types:

- Numeric

- Containers

- Boolean

- Sequence

Note that I don't mention String in the basic data types. This is because of the specific functionality of the strings in Python. Strings are not objects but simple sequences of characters.

Another "missing" data type in Python is the Char. In Python, there is not a specific type for the Char, because it is simply a string with a length of 1. The next sections looks at different data types and explains how you can use them in Python.

Variables in Python

A variable in Python is a container used to store data values. The variable can start with an _ (an underscore), a number, or a letter.

Python doesn't have an explicit type for the variable. This will be cast when you associate the value on the variable.

```
_a = 1
a_ = 3
```

It is possible to cast a variable to a specific type using the constructor of the type you want to create:

```
x = str(3)    # This will create a string
y = int(3)    # This will create an Int
z = float(3)  # This will create a float
```

In Python, variable names are case-sensitive, which means the variables var and Var are two different variables.

Numeric Data Types

Python has three numerical data types:

- Integer

- Float

- Complex number

An integer data type is a number with no decimal point. It can be negative or positive. In Python, an integer is unbounded, and the maximum value for the integer is calculated as *2^(bit size of your computer)-1*. One way to understand the maximum size is to use the `sys.maxsize` command:

```
import sys
sys.maxsize
```

The result of the code is the maximum value of the integer for your computer architecture.

One thing to keep in mind is that the value can be different if you execute the program on a different computer, and this can affect your program, so be very careful when you work with integers in Python.

Float numbers contain a decimal point, and the size of the floating type is defined and represented by a 64-bit double precision.

If you want to know the maximum size of a floating point number, you can use the `sys.float_info` command, which will return the information for the floating number data types.

If you go over the maximum size, Python will return the value `inf`, meaning infinite.

If the number has too many decimal points, Python uses the exponential form, like `1e+20`.

The last type of number you can create in Python is the complex number. This type of number consists of two parts: a *real* part and an *imaginary* part.

To create a complex number in Python, you need to define the real part and the imaginary one. In mathematics, the imaginary part is defined using the *j*. A complex number in Python is `1+0j`.

Another way to create a complex number is to use the `complex()` function from the `cmath` library. The `complex()` function accepts two parameters—the *real part* and the *imaginary part*:

```
import cmath
complex(1,3)
(1+3j)
```

An important note to keep in mind—when you define numbers in Python, the language allows you to use underscores to make the number more readable. For example, you can write the number like so:

```
>>> 1_000_000_000_000
1000000000000
```

Containers

A container is used to store different objects and provide a way to iterate and access the stored objects. Python has four basic containers:

- List

- Tuple

- Dict

- Set

Every container serves different purposes and can impact your program's performance and computational requirements. It is important to understand their differences and choose the right one. The next sections look at the different containers in more detail.

List

A *list* is a mutable sequence of objects. The objects are ordered and indexed by an integer indicating the object's position.

The first element of the list is indicated by the position 0. You can add, remove, and update an element on the list using the specific position of the element. The list is *iterable*, which means that you can use an iterator to read the element present in the list.

The syntax used to create a list in Python is very easy. The element must be written inside square brackets. It is also possible to use the `list()` functions with the elements of the list itself:

```
list_example_1=[1,2,4]
type(list_example_1)
<class 'list'>

list_example_2=list(range(1,5))
type(list_example_2)
<class 'list'>
```

The `list()` function accepts only one parameter. If you want to create a list, you can use the `range()` function, which creates a set of values based on the two parameters passed to the function. Alternatively, you can add elements using the `list()` function between parentheses, such as `list((1,2,3))`.

The `list()` function in Python accepts duplicates. A list can be built with different types. You can create a list that contains strings and numbers. The following example shows an example of a list with different data types:

```
List_2=[1,2,"abc",4]
list_2
[1, 2, 'abc', 4]
```

To access a specific element of a list, you can use the index of the elements. For example, you can access the third element of the list using an index:

```
print(list_2[2])
abc
```

Similarly, you can update the element on the third position with a new value by simply assigning the value to the position of the list:

```
list_2[2] = 5
list_2
[1, 2, 5, 4]
```

Python, like Julia, has some built-in methods, which can be used to manipulate lists. Table 3-1 explains these methods.

Table 3-1. *Built-In List Methods in Python*

Method	Description
append()	Appends the value to the list.
clear()	Deletes all the elements from the array.
copy()	Returns the copy of the list.
extend()	Adds the list, indicated on the parameter, to the end of the actual one.
index()	Searches the list with the value indicated in the parameter and returns the index on the list.
insert()	Inserts a value at the specified position.
pop()	Removes an element at the specified position.
remove()	Removes the first element with the specific value; the value doesn't indicate the position but the value in the list.
reverse()	Reverses the order of the list.
sort()	Sorts the list.

The following examples show how to use this method. The append() method is used to append an element in a list:

```
list_test=[1,3,4,6,5,8]
list_test.append(9)
list_test
[1, 3, 4, 6, 5, 8, 9]
```

The next method in the list is clear(), which removes all the elements in the list:

```
list_test.clear()
list_test
[]
```

Copy is used to return a copy of the list:

```
list_test
[1, 3]
```

```
new_list=list_test.copy()
new_list
[1, 3]
```

The extend() method connects two different lists; the one indicated in the parameter will be added to the end of the list:

```
new_list.extend(list_test)
new_list
[1, 3, 1, 3]
```

There are some cases when you'll want to find the index of a specific value on the array. In this case, you can use the index() method. This method returns the specific index for the first value you indicate in the method:

```
new_list
[1, 3, 1, 3]
new_list.index(3)
1
```

If you want to insert a value in a specific position, you can use the insert() method. This method accepts two parameters—the first one is an index of the list, and the second parameter is the value you want to add:

```
new_list.insert(0,2)
new_list
[2, 1, 3, 1, 3]
```

To remove an element, you can use the pop() method. The method accepts as a parameter the index of the element you want to remove. The method returns the elements removed from the list:

```
new_list.pop(1)
1
new_list
[2, 3, 1, 3]
```

In some cases, you won't know the index of the element. But, you will know the value of the element you want to eliminate from the list. In this case, the removes() method removes the first element containing the value indicated in the parameter from the list:

```
new_list.remove(3)
new_list
[2, 1, 3]
```

The list is unordered. For this purpose, Python has the sort() method. This method sorts the elements in a list:

```
new_list
[2, 1, 3]
new_list.sort()
new_list
[1, 2, 3]
```

If you want reverse the elements in a list, you can use the reverse() method, which will sort the elements from highest to lowest:

```
new_list
[1, 2, 3]
new_list.reverse()
new_list
[3, 2, 1]
```

The len() method returns the length of a list:

```
len(new_list)
3
```

List Comprehension in Python

You can use list comprehension syntax to execute operations in a list. The syntax for creating a list compression is as follows:

```
newlist = [expression for item in iterable if condition == True]
```

The result is a new list. This will leave the old list unchanged and will create a new one.

This can be useful when you want to create a subset of the original list based on some specific parameter. For example, say you want to extract a new list from your main list containing fruit starting with the letter *a* (see Listing 3-1).

Listing 3-1. Example of List Comprehension

```
main_fruit=['apple', 'orange', 'banana', 'grapefruit']

new_fruit = [x for x in main_fruit if x[0]=='a']

print(new_fruit)

print(main_fruit)

['apple']
['apple', 'orange', 'banana', 'grapefruit']
```

As you can see, the original list does not change and a new list is created with the fruit starting with the letter *a*.

Tuples

Tuples are similar to lists; the main difference between tuples and lists is the fact that the tuples are immutable.

To create a tuple, you insert the values inside parentheses. For example, a tuple can be created using this syntax:

```
tuple_example=(1,2)
tuple_example
(1, 2)
```

An alternative syntax for creating a tuple is to use the `tuple()` constructor. Here's an example:

```
tuple_constructor=tuple((1,3,4))
tuple_constructor
(1, 3, 4)
```

Similar to a list, a tuple can maintain different types of data. For example, you can have a char and an integer in the same tuple:

```
tuple_example_new=(1,'a','b',3)
tuple_example_new
(1, 'a', 'b', 3)
```

Because tuples are immutable, they are ideal for storing data you don't need to change, such as the configuration data for the program. It is possible to determine the length of the tuple using the `len()` method:

```
len(tuple_example_new)
4
```

Because tuples are immutable, the built-in methods are only used to count the elements or to search the index of a component. Table 3-2 shows the built-in methods for tuples.

Table 3-2. *The Built-In Elements of a Tuple*

Method	Description
counts()	Counts how many times the tuples contain a specific value.
index()	Searches for an element in the tuple and returns the index.

The `counts()` method is used to indicate how many times a value is present in the tuple:

```
tuple_multiple_elements=('a','a',1,3,'b')
tuple_multiple_elements.count('a')
2
```

The `index()` method is used to search for an element in the tuple and return the index of the first element found:

```
tuple_multiple_elements.index('a')
0
```

If you want to create a tuple with only one element, you need to add a comma after the element. Otherwise, Python won't recognize the structure as a tuple:

```
one_element_tuple=("one",)
type(one_element_tuple)
<class 'tuple'>
```

```
>>> second_element_tuple=("one")
>>> type(second_element_tuple)
<class 'str'>
```

As you can see in the code, if you don't use the comma at the end, Python will not recognize the structure as a tuple but, as a string.

Dictionary

A dictionary in Python is a collection of *key:value pairs*. They are used to store data associated with a specific key.

The *key* is used to associate the *value* in the dictionary. It makes the dictionary different from any of the other collections you've seen up to now.

You can access the value only by the key and not by the value. The syntax to create a dictionary is to use curly brackets followed by the key:value pairs. To indicate the new pairs of values, you use a comma:

```
generative_ai_dictionary={"value_1":"test","value_2":"test2"}
generative_ai_dictionary
{'value_1': 'test', 'value_2': 'test2'}
```

This example creates a dictionary and uses a string as a key for the dictionary.

A key for a dictionary can be a string, a char, an integer, or a float number. The data collected in the dictionary can be different. In a dictionary, for example, you can store numbers, strings, and lists in the same structure.

```
dict_dif_data={"Name":"John", "Surname":"Doe", "Age":20, "Hobbies":
["hicking","reading","programming"]}

dict_dif_data
{'Name': 'John', 'Surname': 'Doe', 'Age': 20, 'Hobbies': ['hicking',
'reading', 'programming']}
```

This example creates a dictionary with different data types, like string, integer, and list.

Dictionaries in Python are changeable and do not allow duplicated keys. Since version 3.7 is ordered, if you use version 3.6 of Python or below, the dictionary is *unordered.*

To build a dictionary, you can use the `dict()` method. In this case, you can just indicate the key:value pair in the constructor or use the equals (=) sign:

```
constructor_dictionary=dict(name="John", surname="Doe")
constructor_dictionary
{'name': 'John', 'surname': 'Doe'}
```

If you want to know the length of the dictionary, you can use the `len()` method, which is similar to what you do for lists and other collections.

Dictionaries are changeable, which means you can use some methods to allow the developer to modify and manipulate the dictionary itself. These methods are shown in Table 3-3.

Table 3-3. *The Dictionary Methods in Python*

Method	Description
`clear()`	Deletes all the elements from the dictionary.
`copy()`	Copies the actual dictionary.
`fromkeys()`	Returns a new dictionary from the keys indicated in the method.
`get()`	Returns the value of the specified key.
`items()`	Returns all the items in the dictionary in the form of a list containing the tuple with the key:value association.
`keys()`	Returns a list containing all the keys from the dictionary.
`pop()`	Removes from the dictionary the elements with the specific key.
`popitem()`	Removes the last inserted key:value item.
`setdefault()`	Returns the specific value indicated with the key. If this doesn't exist in the dictionary, it will create a new one with the indicated value and key.
`update()`	Update the dictionary with the key:value indicated in the method. If this doesn't exist, a new entry will be created.
`values()`	Returns all the values present in the dictionary.

Some of the dictionary methods are quite self-explanatory. Let's see how to use the main methods for the dictionary.

The most used methods in a dictionary are probably keys() and values(), which allow direct access to the key or the value in the dictionary. The key() method is used, for example, when you need to iterate over the dictionary with a loop circle.

```
constructor_dictionary.keys()
dict_keys(['name', 'surname'])
```

As you can see, the keys() method returns the list with all the keys in the dictionary.

---

keys() returns a dict_keys, which is not subscriptable. This means you can't directly use an index to reach the element. In conjunction with the item() method, the values() give you full access to the dictionary element programmatically.

You can easily identify all the values from a dictionary using the values() method. This will return a list with all the values in the array, similar to keys(), and will return a non-subscriptable object:

```
constructor_dictionary.values()
dict_values(['John', 'Doe'])
```

The key() and values() methods both return a non-subscriptable object. If you want to iterate an array, you need to learn something about the items() method, which returns a list with all the items in the array:

```
constructor_dictionary.items()
dict_items([('name', 'John'), ('surname', 'Doe')])
```

As you can see, the list contains a tuple formed with the key:value pairs from the dictionary. The items() method can be used to iterate the dictionary and print the values:

```
constructor_dictionary= dict(name="John", surname="Doe")
for key, value in constructor_dictionary.items():
    print(value)
```

The `items()` method will return a list that contains a tuple of key:value. When Python expands the tuple, you need to associate it with two variables—one for the key and one for the value. If you indicate only one of them, the compiler will return an error.

As you know, the dictionary uses the key to read the data associated with the value. There are two ways to access the value—one is to call the dictionary and the name of the key in square brackets and the other is to use the `get()` method:

```
constructor_dictionary["name"]
'John'
constructor_dictionary.get("name")
'John'
```

Sometimes you might need to return a copy of the dictionary. In this case, you can use the `copy()` method to return a full copy of the original dictionary:

```
new_dict = constructor_dictionary.copy()
new_dict
{'name': 'John', 'surname': 'Doe'}
```

The `fromkeys()` method can be used to generate a new dictionary with the key and the values.

These methods accept the key and the value parameters, which will replace the previous key:value defined and change to a new key:value pair.

The key parameter needs to be an iterable object, for example, a tuple. The `value` parameter is optional and, in this case, is not present. All the keys in the dictionary will be set to None.

```
new_keys=("new_name","new_surname","age")
constructor_dictionary.fromkeys(new_keys,0)
{'new_name': 0, 'new_surname': 0, 'age': 0}
```

The `fromkeys()` method is used to re-create the new key:value in the dictionary. With the new key:value created, you need a method to update the new value in the key. The `update()` method does this:

```
new_dictionary.update({"age":36})
new_dictionary
{'new_name': 0, 'new_surname': 0, 'age': 36}
```

The `pop()`, `popitems()`, and `clear()` methods remove items from the dictionary or completely erase all the elements from the dictionary.

The `pop()` method is used to remove a specific key:value, which means the method needs the key parameter to remove it. The other methods (`popitems()` and `clear()`) don't need any parameters, because they will remove the last element from the dictionary or remove all the elements from the dictionary itself.

Set

A *set* is the fourth built-in collection available in Python. It is used to store multiple items in a single variable.

A set is *unordered, unindexed,* and accepts *unique values.* This means that you can access the data in a set using an index.

You can create a set in Python by using curly brackets, indicating the value you want to add to the set:

```
first_set={"first", "second", "third"}
first_set
{'first', 'third', 'second'}
```

Another way to create a set is to use the `set()` constructor. The syntax is similar to this:

```
set_new=set((1,2,"a"))
set_new
{'a', 1, 2}
```

As with other built-in collections, sets have some methods that can be used to manage them, as shown in Table 3-4.

Table 3-4. *The Set Methods in Python*

Method	Description
`add()`	Adds a new element to the set.
`clear()`	Removes all the elements from a set.
`copy()`	Copies the set into another one.
`difference()`	Returns a set that contains the difference between two or more sets.
`difference_update()`	Removes the differences in the sets, all the elements in common with another one.
`discard()`	Removes a specific item from a set.
`intersection()`	Returns a new set as an intersection between two sets.
`intersection_update()`	Removes the element from the sets if it is not present in the other one.
`isdisjoint()`	Returns `True` if the two sets have an intersection.
`issubset()`	Returns `True` if the set is a subset of the other one.
`issuperset()`	Returns `True` is the set contains the other set.
`pop()`	Removes the last element from the set.
`remove()`	Removes the specified element from the set.
`symmetric_difference()`	Returns the symmetric difference between two sets.
`symmetric_difference_update()`	Inserts the symmetric difference from this set and the other.
`union()`	Returns a new set containing the union of the two sets.
`update()`	Updates the set with the union of this set and the others.

As you can see, the set essentially follows the mathematical rules you have for the set. This makes the set ideal when you want to manage it for mathematical use.

Boolean

Boolean in Python is essentially similar to any other language. It can have only two values—True or False. You can create a Boolean in two ways:

- Create a variable and assign it a value of True or False.

- Use the bool constructor.

If you use the bool() constructor, it is important to note that the value will be True for any number different than 0, and False for 0:

```
bol_number=bool(0)
bol_number
False

bol_number=bool(15)
bol_number
True
bol_number=bool(-1)
bol_number
True
```

The Boolean is normally used to evaluate the difference between two statements, such as in an if..else constructor.

For convention, when you create a Boolean using bool, a True statement is indicated by 1 and a False is indicated by 0.

Sequence Data Types (aka Strings)

Python is written using C and shares the construction of a string. In Python, a string is essentially a list of characters. It doesn't have a specific char type, because the char is a string with only one element.

Strings can be created in Python using single or double quotes, but when you print them out, Python will show them in single quotes.

```
double_quote = "Test double quote"
double_quote
'Test double quote'

single_quote='Test single quote'
single_quote
'Test single quote'
```

You can create a quote inside a string, but you need to use the quote type that you didn't use to create the string. This example used double quotes to create the string, so it would use the single quotes:

```
quote_inside_string="example 'of quote' inside the string"
quote_inside_string
"example 'of quote' inside the string"
```

In Python, it is possible to use the triple quotes syntax to create multiline comments in your code. This syntax is useful when you want to add comments.

```
test_multiline="""Multiline
... comment
... example"""

test_multiline
'"Multiline\ncomment\nexample'
```

The string in Python is a sequence of characters, and because of that, you can access a string's character using the index position.

```
character_string="Test string position"
character_string[5]
's'
```

In this case, you read the character in the fifth position of the string itself. You can use a simple for loop to access to all the characters in the string:

```
test_loop="Test"

for ch in test_loop:
    print(ch)
```

```
T
e
s
t
```

This code will print all the characters in the string, which is another useful way to check if a string is contained within another one.

This is done using the `in` keyword. If the command returns `True`, the string is contained in another string; if it returns `False`, it is not contained in a string.

```
first_string="Test in string"
second_string="in"
second_string in first_string
True
```

You can also determine if the substring is not contained in another string. You can do this using the `not in` keyword:

```
first_string="Test in String"
second_string="of"
second_string not in first_string
True
```

The substring check is useful when you're executing a conditional statement, such as an `if..then`.

Conditional Statements

In Python, conditional statements work similarly to other languages. A conditional statement is used to evaluate a condition and adapt the code based on the results.

An `if` condition uses some logical condition collected from mathematics. This condition is used to evaluate the conditional statements. The logical conditions are listed in Table 3-5.

Table 3-5. *The Logical Conditions in Python*

Conditions	Description
==	Equal condition
>=	Greater than or equal to
!=	Not equal to
<	Less than
>	Greater than
<=	Less than or equal to

Here's an example of a conditional statement in Python:

```
a =1
b =3

if a>b:
  print("a is greater than b")
elif a<b:
  print("a is less than b")
else:
  print("a is equal to b")
```

The code will print the statement for the condition based on the a and b variables. In this case, the output will be a is less than b.

The elif condition is the "else if" condition, and it works similarly to other languages. It evaluates the condition and prints a statement. If you want to see how the different else..ifs are evaluated, just change the a and b variables and see how the print statement changes.

Functions

Functions are used to organize code in reusable blocks. The function is the building block of every program and can help to better structure the code. The syntax for creating a function in Python is as follows:

```
def <function name>(<parameter1>,<parameter2>,…<parameter_n>)
```

Python doesn't use a specific word to close functions. You don't have to add the `return` keyword to close a function. Here's a basic example of a Python function:

```
def sum(a,b):
    return a+b

print(sum(2,2))
```

This code will execute a simple sum of two numbers. The function uses the `return` keyword, which ensures that the value is available outside the function.

Some languages distinguish between methods and functions. A method is essentially a function that does not return a value, whereas a function returns a value. In Python, you can make this distinction by simply omitting the `return` keyword.

In Python, you can have an arbitrary number of parameters for the function. This is indicated by the *argv and **kwargs keywords. The difference between the two keywords is how the parameters are created.

The *argv keyword is essentially a list that contains several parameters, whereas the **kwargs keyword is a key:value list of parameters. This distinction is important for understanding how to access the values of the parameters in your function. Listing 3-2 shows the *argv keyword in use.

Listing 3-2. An Example of Usage or Variable Arguments

```
def variable_value(*argv):
  for arg in argv:
    print(arg)

variable_value(1,2,3,4,5,6)
```

You can read the value of the *argv parameters like any other list. You can send an arbitrary number of parameters and read the index position of the parameters.

The **kwargs returns the value in a key:value list. Listing 3-3 shows an example.

Listing 3-3. An Example of Using **kwargs

```python
def keypair_variable(**kwargs):
  for key, value in kwargs.items():
    print(key, value)

keypair_variable(name='James', age=25)
```

The first line of the comment in a function is important for creating the documentation. This is called the docustring and can be shown when you use the __ doc__ method associated with the function. Listing 3-4 shows an example.

Listing 3-4. An Example of a Docustring in Python

```python
def example_of_docustring():
  """This is an example of docustring in python"""
  Return

print(example_of_docustring.__doc__)
```

Anonymous Functions in Python

Anonymous functions are created without an associated name. Anonymous functions are created using the lambda keyword. Listing 3-5 shows an example of how a normal function can be written using a lambda function.

Listing 3-5. A Lambda Function Example

```python
def cube(x):
  return x*x*x

# lambda function for cube
cube_lambda = lambda x : x*x*x

print(cube(3))

print(cube_lambda(3))
```

This code shows how to translate a normal function into an anonymous one. The keyword lambda creates the anonymous function, then you associate the anonymous variable with a variable and can use the variable as a reference to the function.

As any other type of function, you can pass multiple variables to a Lambda function:

```
x = lambda first, second: first * second

print(x(2,2))

4
```

Anonymous functions are not completely anonymous, because if you need to pass some parameters to them, you need to associate the function with a variable. This makes it possible for the code to send the parameter for the function itself. The real power of this type of function is when you use it inside another function. You can use the variable defined in the scope of the function as a parameter for the anonymous function and nest another function inside the main one.

Loops in Python

Python has two different types of loops:

- While

- For

There is a difference between the two loops and this indicates how many loops will be executed. The while loop will be executed until the condition is true. The for loop is used to iterate over a sequence.

This difference between while and for is important because it can influence the number of loops you execute in your code, and this in turn can impact the computational efficiency of your code. This difference becomes more evident when you analyze the different syntaxes used to create the loops. Listings 3-6 and 3-7 show an example of these two loops.

Listing 3-6. A for Loop in Python

```
for_loops = ["one","two","three","four","five"]
for x in for_loops:
  print(x)
```

The `for`-loop syntax is quite simple and doesn't require any indexing variable to be declared. The code will print this result:

```
one
two
three
four
five
```

The variable x iterates the list, defined after the keyword in. The variable will be associated with an element of the array, which means when the array reaches the last element, the loop will end.

The `while` loop has a different behavior. It requires that an indexing variable be declared before the loop. The variable must be increased during the loop, which means that the loop can execute one last iteration before exiting. Listing 3-7 shows an example of this process.

Listing 3-7. The while Loop in Python

```
i=0

while i < 6:
  print("While" + str(i))
  i += 1
```

The result of the loop is as follows:

```
While0
While1
While2
While3
While4
While5
```

As you can see from the result, if you start from the value 0, the `while` loop will execute an iteration more than is needed.

It is possible to interrupt a `while` or a `for` loop early using the `break` keyword, which will immediately interrupt the execution of the loop. Listing 3-8 shows an example of this syntax.

Listing 3-8. An Example of Using the break Keyword

```
for_loops = ["one","two","three","four","five"]
i=0
for x in for_loops:
  print(x)
  i+=1
  if i == 3:
    break
```

The result of the Listing 3-8 is as follows:

```
one
two
three
```

The for loop in this case will be interrupted after three iterations. The break conditions are the same in the while loop. Listing 3-9 shows this syntax.

Listing 3-9. The break in the while Loop

```
i=0
while  i<10:
  print(i)
  i+=1
  if i==3:
    break
```

Another keyword used in the loops is continue. In this case, the next action in the loop is executed. Listing 3-10 shows how the continue keyword affects loops.

Listing 3-10. The continue Keyword in a Loop

```
i=0
while  i<10:
  i+=1
  if i==3:
    continue
  print(i)
```

The result of this code will be as follows:

```
1
2
4
5
6
7
8
9
10
```

As you can see, the result does not have the number 3. This is because the `continue` keyword skips the rest of the loop and moves the loop to the next iteration.

Conclusion

This chapter introduced the Python language. The goal of this chapter was to introduce the basics of the language, and explain Python functionality. Compressing an entire language into one chapter is impossible, and this chapter is just an introduction. The rest of the book shows more Python features and expands your knowledge of the language.

## CHAPTER 4

Introduction to Generative Artificial Intelligence

The previous chapters provided a short introduction to AI, followed by a short introduction to Julia and Python. This chapter expands your knowledge of generative artificial intelligence by going deeper and defining the necessary theory, including some basic examples, so that you can learn how to build your own generative AI model.

Generative AI Is All Around

If you think a minute about what you do every day, you will probably realize that you are using one of the generative AI models.

During your job, you probably write emails, and if English is not your language, you probably use software similar to Grammarly to help correct your grammar. You are using a generative AI model, Grammarly.

You might use Copilot to generate images from text or to synthesize notes. In this case, you are using a generative AI model.

Nowadays, if you mention generative AI, people immediately think of a LLM model, such as ChatGPT from OpenAI. Or they can think about Llama by Meta, or Gemini by Google Deepmind. All these models are applications of the generative artificial intelligence. Of course, they are very complex and some of them, like Gemini and VEO, are *multimodal models*. All of these models, if you go deep into the core of the system, have the same basics. The rest of the chapter explains these basics so that you can use available models as well as start to build your own.

A *multimodal model* is capable of processing information from different sources. A multimodal model uses information from different sources, for example, images, text, and audio, to generate new data. An example of multimodal is the DALL-E, where you enter data at a prompt and the model will create the corresponding image. The multimodal model expands the generative capacity of the model, adding to the model the capacity to collect information from different sources.

Generative AI improved greatly in December 2018, when NVIDIA released the first version of StyleGAN. It gained media attention, and with the explosion of ChatGPT by OpenAI, it started to be a media phenomenon.

Deep Generative Modelling

If you wanted to describe a generative model to a child, you could use an analogy, which is the similar process they might use to draw an image based on a description you tell them, such as when you ask them to draw a picture of an airplane.

If you want to simplify the concept of generative modelling to its bare bones, that's it—generative modelling generates data based on previous knowledge, similar to the process a child uses to draw an airplane. A generative model uses the knowledge to "draw" new data.

Chapter 1 introduced the difference between the generative model and the discriminative model. A *generative model* is a statistical class used to generate new data.

A class of statistical models uses a joint probability conditional distribution, $P(X, Y)$. The distribution is calculated on a given *observable variable X* and the *target variable Y*. This model generates a random outcome of an observation X.

Understanding this basic theory is necessary to understand how generative AI works. It is not necessary to be an expert of probability, but you do need to understand some basic terminology. The first step is to understand these key terms:

- Sample space

- Density function

- Parametric modelling

- Maximum likelihood

Sample Space

Sample space is one of the core terms of generative AI. A *sample space* is the entire set of values that an observation can make. Imagine you want to generate some data similar to Figure 4-1.

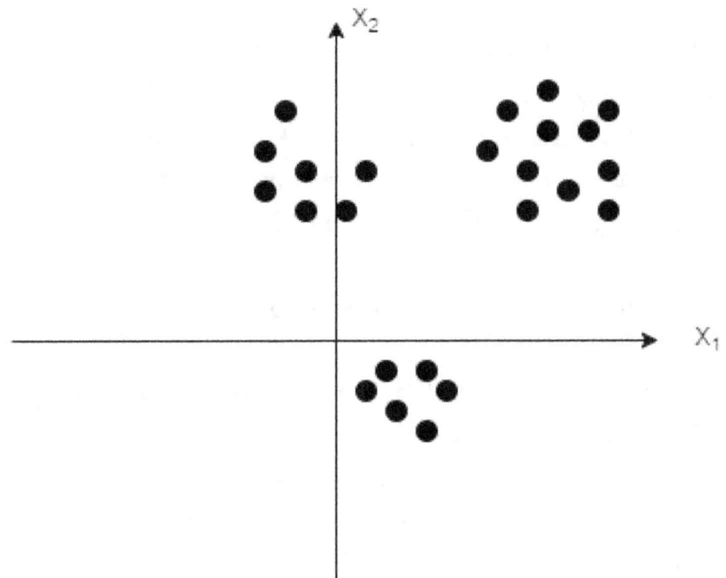

Figure 4-1. *An example of data you want to generate*

To generate new data, you need to *learn* how the data is distributed, and to do that you need to *observe* all the data. The data you observe is essentially the *sample space.*

The sample space is the entire set of observations. In this case, all the points in the graph. In this case, we can define the sample space X in this way: $X = (x_1, x_2)$.

Density Function

The *density function, or probability density function,* maps all the points for the sample space. These will be mapped in numbers between 0 and 1. The function is represented in this way: $p(X)$.

The density function is a well-defined probability distribution, and the function's sum between all the numbers must be equal to 1. In the previous example, the sum of all the points in the axis must equal 1, and all the points outside the range must equal 0.

Observing the data, there is only one density function, called p_{data}, that generates all the data in the datasets.

But you can have an infinite number of density functions to estimate the p_{data}. This function can be called $p_{model}(x)$. To determine the $p_{model}(x)$, you use a technique called *parametric modelling*.

Parametric Modelling

Parametric modelling is used to find the density function of the data. This technique uses a finite number of parameters, θ.

The function can be described in this way: $p_\theta(x)$. The parameters θ are essentially all the data you need to represent, which in this example is all the data in Figure 4-1. The data can be identified by the coordinates x1 and x2 from the bottom left and top right. In this case, there are four parameters: $\theta = (\theta_1, \theta_2, \theta_3, \theta_4)$.

The parameters θ_1 and θ_2 are the bottom-left coordinates and the parameters θ_3 and θ_4 are the top-right coordinates.

The parameter θ must be calculated, because you need to be sure the parameter is a valid one. To do that, you can use a function called *likelihood*. The *likelihood* of the parameter θ is a function that is used to measure the plausibility of the parameter based on the observed point X. The function is defined in this way:

$$L(\theta|X) = p_\theta(X)$$

The function is used to calculate the likelihood of θ given the observation X, and the result is the value of the density function for the specific point x.

When you have an entire dataset, you need to rewrite the function to consider all the observations. The function can be written like so:

$$L(\theta|X) = \Pi_{x \in X} p_\theta(X)$$

This function is very computationally expensive because the Π symbol indicates a sequence of multiplication for every observation x in the dataset X. To reduce the computation complexity, you use a different formula called *log-likelihood*. The function is as follows:

$$l(\theta|X) = \sum_{x \in X} \log p_\theta(X)$$

I don't want to go deep and explain the statistical reason behind the definition of the likelihood, it is enough to understand that you define the likelihood of a set of parameters θ to be equal to the probability of seeing the data under the parameter θ.

In Figure 4-1, if you observe the data on the left side of the graph, there is 0 probability that you will draw data on the right side of the graph, because the observation x is only on one side. This means if you try to evaluate a data point on the right side, the function will give you a value equal to 0.

Parametric modelling should find the optimal value for the set of parameters θ that maximizes the likelihood of the observing dataset X. This is easily understandable, as you want to generate data that can appear within the real observations and not data that can't ever be in the observation. For example, if you want to generate data about the temperature in London in November, it would be unrealistic to generate 40 degrees Celsius. In this case, you can use a technique called *maximum likelihood estimation*.

Maximum Likelihood Estimation

The *maximum likelihood estimation, MLE*, is the technique used to determine the value of the parameters model. This is indicated by $\hat{\theta}$. This function represents the MLE:

$$\hat{\theta} = argmax_\theta L(\theta|X)$$

This technique evaluates the density function, which most likely explains the observed data X. For the aim of the book this definition is enough; I don't want to go deep into the statistical definition, which is very complex and unnecessary for this book.

Your First Generative Model

Up to now, I have talked about the generative model in a complex, probabilistic way. You saw the basic term used to generate the data, but exactly how can you generate new data? How can you use all these formulas to generate it? A simple example can explain the process. In this example, you need to analyze sales from a bakery and try to understand how to produce new flavors for the cakes to improve sales.

The first step of generating new data is to observe the actual data. To do that, you need to collect information about the cake sales. In this case, you collect a dataset of 100 observations and define the observations as *N=100*. The observations represent the sales. They have four features (`cakeFlavors`, `cakeType`, `cakeSize`, and `filling`). Table 4-1 shows an example of this data.

Table 4-1. *The First Ten Observations from the Cake Dataset*

ID	cakeFlavor	cakeType	cakeSize	filling
1	Strawberry	Round	18	Cream
2	Cream	Square	20	Jam
3	Lemon	Round	10	VanillaCream
4	Chocolate	Round	20	Cream
5	RedVelvet	Square	10	Jam
6	SaltedCaramel	Square	20	None
7	Vanilla	Round	25	Chocolate
8	Blackberry	Square	15	Jam
9	Oreo	Round	10	Cream
10	Neapolitan	Square	30	none

The dataset shows ten different flavors for the cake, (*Strawberry, Cream, Lemon, Chocolate, RedVelvet, SaltedCaramel, Vanilla, Blackberry, Oreo,* and *Neapolitan*). There are also two types of cake (*round* and *square*), six sizes (*10, 15, 18, 20, 25,* and *30*) and five types of filling (*Cream, Jam, Chocolate, VanillaCream,* and *none*).

Based on all the observations, you can have 600 (10 x 2 x 6 x 5) combinations of these five features. These various combinations represent the 600 points in the sample space. As you know, the goal of a generative model is to understand the observations and build a model that can mimic the observations of the data.

The observations of the dataset can be p_{data}, and the goal of this model is to find all the possible *density functions* that represent the data. You identify the function you want to find as p_{model}.

At this point, you need to generate some new data, which is done by assigning a probability to each possible combination. This probability is generated based on the actual observations. Based on these observations, you have a parametric model with $\theta = 400$ parameters, one for each point.

Based on the parameters, this example uses parametric modelling to estimate all the parameters. In this case, you try to estimate $(\theta_1, .., \theta_{400})$.

This is a specific type of parametric modelling, and it's called *multinomial distribution*. You will estimate the maximum likelihood for every parameter. The parameter will be evaluated based on the number of times it's found the data in the observation. This helps estimate the amount of time every combination was observed in the dataset, because the more often the elements are present in the dataset, the greater probability they are present in the generated data.

Based on the data, no combination has a 0 probability of being present. This makes it very difficult to generate new data because essentially you need to generate all the possible combinations. This makes the generations very complex. To reduce this complexity, you can use another technique, called *Naïve Bayes*.

With Naïve Bayes parametric modelling, you can make a simple assumption that helps drastically reduce the number of parameters that need to be estimated.

To understand how Naïve Bayes works, you need to understand how the features are evaluated for the generation. Parametric modelling generates new data and correlates all the information. Because all the data is correlated, the `cakeType` and `cakeFlavor` are connected, so you can generate the data without using this information. You can call these features x_y and x_k.

The Naïve Bayes approach makes the *naïve* assumption that each feature x_y is *independent* of every other feature x_k. In simple terms, the `cakeType` is not related to the `cakeFlavor`. The approach with the Naïve Bayes can be represented in this way:

$$p(x_y|x_k) = p(x_y)$$

This formula is the Naïve Bayes assumption. You can apply this assumption by using the chain rule of probability. The final result of the formula is as follows:

$$p(x) = \Pi_{k=1}^{K} p(x_k)$$

This formula helps estimate how many parameters you need to create this model. The Naïve Bayes model can learn the data structure and use it to generate new examples not present in the original dataset. This is because you calculate the probability of observations you didn't see in the dataset; for example, you can have a probability of a new observation like cake with this observation:

```
cakeType = Square, cakeSize = 30, cakeFlavor = Strawberry, filling =
chocolate
```

This type of data is not present in the observation, but Naïve Bayes can help highlight this data. You will see in the rest of the book how to use and generate the data, for now is important to understand the basics behind the generative model.

How Important Is Probability in Generative AI?

Suppose you tried to simplify the machine learning model. In that case, you can reduce it to a simple mathematical model that describes how various kinds of data are related.

Normally this mathematical model—in the case of the prediction model for example when we model linear regression—is used to define the probability of seeing the same data structure in the future. Imagine for example that you created a model used to forecast housing prices in a specific town.

The model will learn the probability of seeing a specific combination of features and associate it with a specific price. Table 4-2 shows an example of how this data might look.

Table 4-2. *An Example of Extracted Housing Prices*

ID	Bedrooms	Bathroom	Type	Garden	Price	Zone
1	3	2	Semi-Detached	Rear	300.000	Zone1
2	2	1	Apartment	No	150000	Zone1
3	2	2	Detached	Rear/Front	300000	Zone2
4	3	3	Apartment	No	250000	Zone2
5	4	2	Detached	Front	350000	Zone3

As you can see from Table 4-2, different factors change the price of a house, and the mathematical model will try to associate a probability to every specific condition. To be specific, the model calculates the *likelihood* of seeing the combination.

In the data extracted in Table 4-2, there are six features. For every feature, you can calculate the probability of seeing it in the dataset. You can calculate the likelihood of having a house with three bedrooms in this way:

$$P(X = 3) = \frac{2}{6} = 33.33\%$$

The letter *P* denotes the *probability of*. In this case, the *P* denotes the probability of having three bedrooms.

This example has a limited number of observations, only six, which means the probability of having a three-bedroom house is essentially a third of the observations. For example, the dataset doesn't have an observation with a one-bedroom house, but this doesn't mean one doesn't exist. This highlights important rules for machine learning. If you want to generate new data, you need to have a dataset large enough to completely describe the phenomena you want to address.

This can be explained using the Three Kolmogorov's Axioms, which were proposed in 1933 by the mathematician Andrey Kolmogorov. They are the core concepts of probability theory. The three axioms say:

- **First axiom:** The probability contains real numbers; there are no negative numbers.

- **Second axiom:** At least one result in the same space will occur with a probability of 1. In other words, viewing an experiment will result in an outcome.

- **Third axiom:** In a sample space with an unlimited number of disconnected events, the probability of a union of events is equal to the sum of all event probabilities.

These axioms establish the basic rule of probability and is important when talking about machine learning and deep learning. The first axiom, for example, is used to generate a finite number between 0 and 1 when you want to define the outcome of a probability (you do this using, for example, a softmax function).

The second axiom ensures that based on the dataset of the observation, at least one combination of data that appears in the dataset can be generated.

The third axiom is probably the most important. It normalizes the outcomes in the range 0-1 because the axiom will ensure that all the results of observation must be unique to a specific class. For example, based on the previous house dataset, you will have only one result, a three-bedroom house. When you receive new data for the classification, you can't have two different classes at the same time, for example a three-bedroom and a two-bedroom house.

What is described up to now are essentially the basic rules of classification or regression. But when we talk about modelling data, we use *conditional probability*.

Probability of Generating New Data

In generative AI, we are not interested in understanding the probability of seeing a specific observation, but we are interested in understanding the condition that makes this observation available.

Using the example of the housing prices, if you need to generate new data, you are not interested in understanding what the price for a three-bedroom house will be in a specific area, but you are interested in understanding the *condition* that creates a specific price. This is called the conditional probability.

You can define the conditional probability as *the probability of having the outcome y given the input x*. More formally, the formula for a conditional probability is as follows:

$$P(Y \vee X)$$

Understanding when the probability Y happens based on the event X is important, but it can't alone be used to define new data.

In Table 4-2, for example, the price of a house reaches \$300,000 in some cases with three bedrooms and in some cases with two bedrooms. The difference is another condition, and this introduces another important concept of the probability needed for generating new data—*joint probability*. Joint probability is the statistical measure that calculates the likelihood of two events occurring together simultaneously. More formally, joint probability is as follows:

$$P(X \cap Y)$$

Where the symbol $\cap$ indicates the intersection of the event X and Y. It's important to understand the difference between conditional and joint probability. Joint probability only calculates the likelihood that both events occur. On the other hand, conditional probability calculates the probability that a specific event will occur. Another important theorem of probability to keep in mind is Bayes Theorem.

Bayes Theorem

When talking about a machine learning algorithm, we distinguish between two specific families:

- Discriminative

- Generative

A *discriminative model* is essentially a model that tries to predict an outcome based on past observations. More formally, a discriminative model attempts to learn a direct connection between the data X and the outcome Y.

A *generative model,* on the other hand, tries to learn when the condition of the input data X and the outcome Y will appear. A generative model doesn't try to predict the outcome, but based on the outcome, tries to reproduce the input.

Bayes Theorem was named after the mathematician Thomas Bayes. It gives a mathematical rule that can be used to invert the conditional probability, which allows you to find the probability of a cause given its effect. Bayes Theorem is defined in this way:

$$P(X|Y) = \frac{P(Y|X)P(X)}{P(Y)}$$

In plain English, the formula can be expressed as follows:

$$Posterior = \frac{(Likelihood)(Prior)}{(Evidence)}$$

- *Posterior* is the revised or updated probability of an event occurring after taking into consideration the new data.

- Likelihood measures the probability of observing the specific data.

- Prior is the assumed probability distribution before some evidence is taken into the count.

- Evidence, or *marginal likelihood,* represents the probability of generating the observed example.

Let's consider an example to understand how Bayes Theorem works. Table 4-2 shows a series of observations of housing prices. The observations have some features and all these features give you an idea about the potential price of the house.

If you want to define a discriminative model to predict the price of a house, *posterior* is the observed price, where the *likelihood* is the condition for the specific price. For example, for the number of bedrooms or the zone, the *prior* can be for example another feature, like the type of the house. All these variables are calculated by dividing all the information by the *evidence,* which indicates the number of houses that have that price. The result is the probability of observing the specific price for some specific variables.

The importance of Bayes Theorem is in the fact that the evidence can change the value of the probability. From the observations, for example, the probability of a single-bedroom house costing $300,000 is 0. However, if you expand the observation, you can start to observe this condition and then the probability moves from 0 to, for example, 0.1%.

Generative modelling attempts to learn a joint distribution of the labels and the data input, in this context, Bayes Theorem can help you find a posterior based on the prior observations and the likelihood of the observation. In the case of generative modelling, the model tries to find *latent variables.*

In statistics, a *latent variable* is a variable that can be inferred indirectly through a mathematical model from the observable variables. To put this in simple words, a latent value is something that you cannot directly observe. It is derived from a series of observations. For example, this could be the quality of life in a particular zone, which can be measured and can influence housing prices in Table 4-2.

A generative model will use Bayes Theorem to learn the joint distribution of the data. This can be done because the Bayes Theorem can be rewritten in this way:

$$P(X|Y) = \frac{P(X,Y)}{P(X)}$$

In this case, you can use Bayes Theorem to calculate the posterior, the probability of having the output, based on the joint probability of seeing other data. To use the example in Table 4-2, the latent variable can be the good name of zone 1, and based on that, the model can generate new data and put a new $300,000 one-bedroom house in zone 1. This will have a lower probability, but the probability can improve when new observations and new data become available.

Different Types of Generative Models

Chapter 1 explained the four main types of generative modelling and discussed a short introduction about the different ways they generate data. Before you start to implement some of this model, this section goes a bit deeper into these definitions and the theory behind these types. It also introduces some basic usage in the domain of deep learning.

Autoregressive Model

An autoregressive model is a family of machine learning algorithms that predict the next component in a sequence by taking measurements from previous inputs in the sequence.

This type of model is very useful when working with recursive data. Autoregressive models are an important part of large language models (LLMs).

Autoregressive models are also used in image synthesis, such as with PixelRNN and PixelCNN, where the autoregressive model is used to generate images, pixel by pixel. How can an autoregressive model learn the data? Imagine the case of an LLM that will be trained on several English sentences. The model learns that the word "there" will always be followed by the word "is". This learning is used by the model when generating new data, in this case, when the model puts the word "there," it will add the word "is" forming "there is".

In the field of machine learning, an RNN has similar structure to an autoregressive model, and there are a lot of similarities. The next section shows how to write the most simple autoregressive model, an RNN.

Autoregressive Models with RNN

A recurrent neural network (RNN) is a well-known architecture capable of working with sequential data. An RNN basically works similarly to a feedforward network, but this specific type of network can accept two types of weight in inputs. The first type of weight is the normal input for the network, the data you want to learn, and the second set of weights is the output of the previous recurrent neuron. In its simple state, a recurrent neuron can be represented as shown in Figure 4-2.

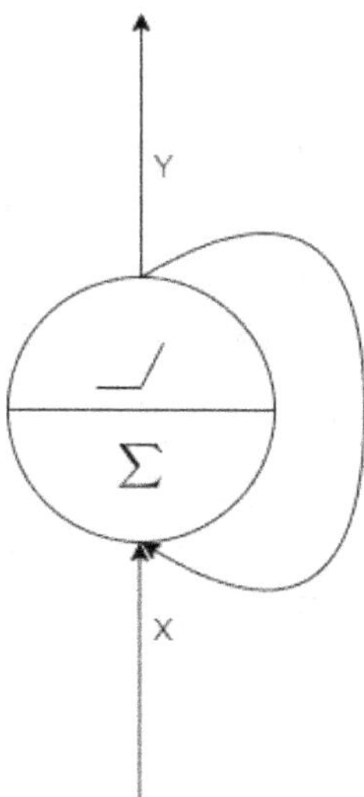

Figure 4-2. *A single recurrent neuron*

As you can see, the output of the neuron is sent back as input. This is a very basic recurrent neural network. Of course, to be effective a neural network must have more than one neuron and work with sequential data. A more complex network is represented in Figure 4-3.

Figure 4-3 shows what is called an *unrolled network through time*. The network is essentially exploded using a specific time frame, t, and you can see how the output of the previous steps is used as input for the actual steps. In the figure, t-2 is the input for the steps t-1. This makes the recurrent neural network "remember" the previous input of the data.

Since the output of the previous neuron is used as input for the actual neuron, the RNN starts to have some kind of memory. In this case, it's called a *memory cell* or a simple *cell*. Figure 4-2 shows an example of the simplest cell possible. RNNs are important in the context of generative modelling, because they can remember a small amount of data previously inserted into the network. This capability makes them the perfect candidate for text translation from one language to another, or for text generation. But to do that, you need to understand another important concept of RNNs—the *long short-term memory* (LSTM).

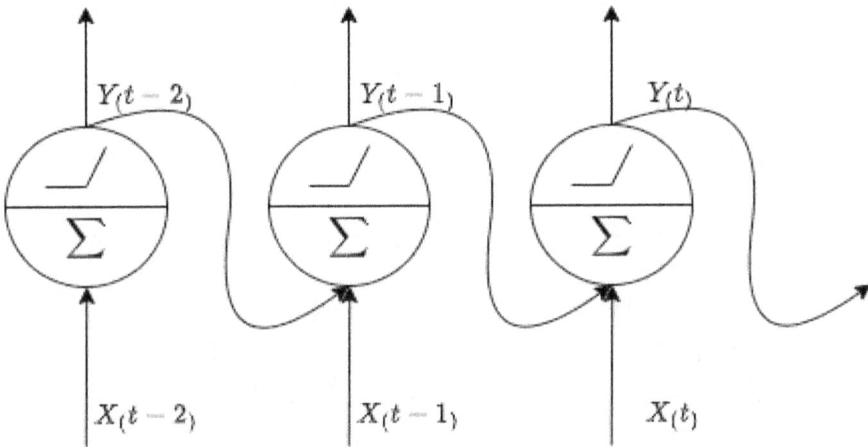

Figure 4-3. *An unrolled recurrent neural network*

Long Short-Term Memory

RNNs can "remember" a small amount of data, typically around ten previous inputs, but this can be smaller depending on the type of data. This is a limitation, particularly in complex tasks like text generation. To improve this capability, researchers introduced what is called long short-term memory (LSTM).

The idea behind the LSTM is that the network can learn what to store in the long-term state, what to throw away, and finally what to read from it. The structure of LSTM is represented in Figure 4-4.

LSTM has as input two vectors, indicated as h_t and c_t. h_t is the short-term state and c_t is the long-term state. Figure 4-3 shows the expanded LSTM cell. As you can see, the c_{t-1} cell moves from left to right. The first gate interacts with the long-term cell, c_{t-1}, which is a *forget gate*. This gate is used to remove some memory, because we will immediately add more memory. This is done by the addition operation, and the memory added is directly collected by the input gate I_t. The output is then sent directly without any more transformation, and this becomes c_t. At the end of the operation, some memories are removed and some memories are added back in.

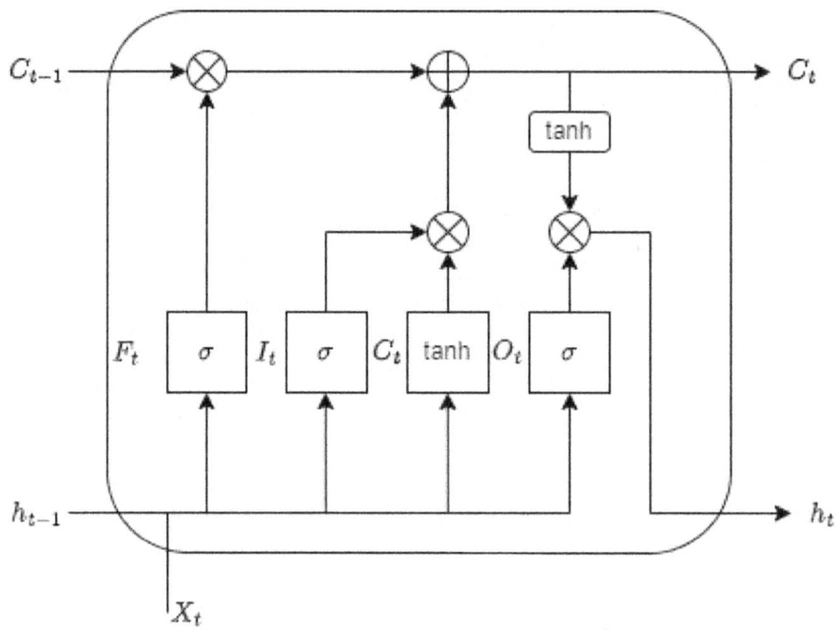

Figure 4-4. *A structure of an LSTM cell*

Identifying which memories are added in the long term and which are removed is determined by some specific gate.

The *forget gate, F_t,* is used to identify which memories can be removed in the actual long term. At this point, two new gates enter into action to decide what memory should be added to the long-term memory. This is done by the I_t, the *input gate,* and from the C_t, a cell that applies a *tanh* activation function. The tanh function is used because the function will have a result between -1 and 1.

LSTM plays a vital role in all the modern architecture for text generation, because of its capacity to learn more data from past sequences. This improves the capacity to remember the data processed before and then have a better understanding of the data that needs to be generated. Before closing this section, it is important to understand the different types of processing data that an RNN can use.

Different RNN Output

As you learned in the previous section, an RNN can simultaneously have a sequence of inputs and produce a sequence of outputs. Figure 4-2 shows the basic capability of an RNN. This type of input/output combination is called a *sequence-to-sequence network,* and this type of configuration is very useful when you want to predict time series events.

Another type of configuration is called a *sequence-to-vector network*. In this configuration, the input is a sequence of data, like the previous one, but it ignores any other output and just considers the last one. This type of configuration is useful when you want to do sentiment analysis, where the network will analyze the entire sentence before scoring the result.

You can also have a *vector-to-sequence network*. In this case, you send to the network the same input as a vector over and over again, and the output will be a sequence at every time frame. This kind of architecture is useful when you need to label an image. The input can be the piece of an image and the RNN will provide the label evolved based on the piece of information received.

The last kind of configuration is predominantly used in the field of generative AI, in particular in text generation. This configuration mixes two other kinds of configurations. The first part of the configuration is a sequence-to-vector network, called the *encoder*.

The encoder is followed by a vector-to-sequence network, called the *decoder*. This *encoder-decoder* architecture is used to generate new data. It's used when you want to translate from one language to another. In this case, the encoder will collect the information about the sentence in the original language, and the decoder will use the input to translate the entire sentence.

Recall that the autoregressive model learns the probability of having the word "is" after the word "there." During the translation, the decoder finds the translated word with "there" and immediately will add the word "is." RNN is widely used for NLP (Natural Language Processing). The goal of the book is not to introduce and fully explain RNN, but to give you a basic understanding of this architecture. This is important in particular when dealing with *transformers*, an evolution of RNN and the backbone of many LLMs.

Flow-Based Networks and Residual Networks

A flow-based model is a generative model that explicitly models the probability distribution leveraging *normalizing flow*. Normalizing flow is a statistical method that uses the *change-of-variable law* of the probability, which transforms a simple distribution into a complex one.

I do not discuss the math and the statistics behind this because it's out of the scope of the boo and requires a deep knowledge of statistics.

One of the most common applications of a flow-based network is *ResNet*. This type of architecture uses a *residual connection* or *skip connection*. In this architecture, the weight layer learns the residual functions concerning the layer inputs. This architecture was designed for image recognition in 2015, and the core idea behind it is to address the issue of vanishing/exploding gradients.

When you train a neural network, the goal is to make it model the target function $h(x)$. In the ResNet architecture, you add an input X, which forces the neural network to learn the function $f(x) = h(x) - x$, when normally the neural network would learn only $h(x)$. This is called *residual learning*, and Figure 4-5 shows this behavior.

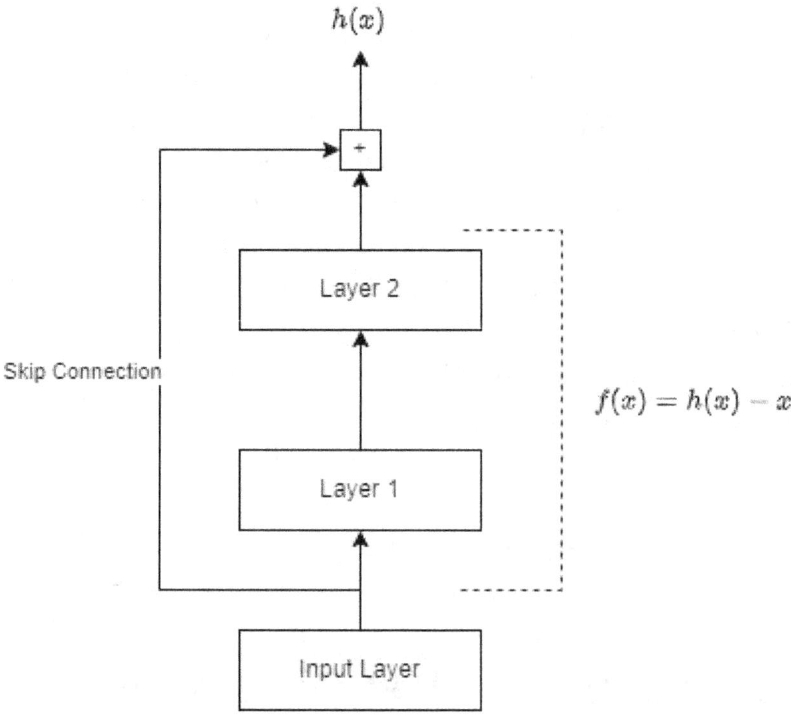

Figure 4-5. *The ResNet skip connection and the residual learning*

As you can see, the skip connection with some layer—between the input and the activation function—improves the performance in the sense of training and reduces the problem with the exploding gradient.

The importance of the residual network is that every transformer uses a residual network layer. It would otherwise be impossible to completely train the transformer.

Transformers: "Attention Is All You Need"

Transformers are one of the landmarks in the science of AI. This architecture was introduced in 2017 by eight Google scientists and revolutionized deep learning and artificial intelligence in general.

The idea of the transformers was introduced in the 2017 paper, "Attention Is All You Need," by Vaswani, et al. The transformer was inspired by the RNN and is one of the most versatile architectures in the field of AI. In its simple form, a transformer is an encoder-decoder architecture, where the input is encoded and decoded as output. But a transformer is more than that.

Transformers are used in different fields, in particular with RNN and CNN. Probably the most known use of transformers is the LLM model, such as GPT and Llama. The architecture of the transformer is represented in Figure 4-6.

At its core, it uses what is called the *attention* mechanism, and in particular the *self-attention mechanism.* This is probably the most powerful improvement in the field of AI. This mechanism helps the neural network focus on only the important part of the sequence of data.

The transformer was developed to solve the problem of *sequence transduction,* or *neural machine translation.* This type of task is used to transform an input sequence into another input sequence, such as translating from one language to another.

In RNN, the encoding/decoding configuration accepts as input a set of data. When all the data is collected, the output will be sent on a specific time frame. This is a seq2seq architecture and is used when you want to translate a sentence from one language to another. Recall that an RNN can memorize only short sentences, which makes such a translation imperfect. To prevent this issue, an attention mechanism can help.

To better understand an *attention* mechanism, you need to understand the basic idea behind how an RNN is used for transduction. The RNN selects some hidden state and uses it to translate the data.

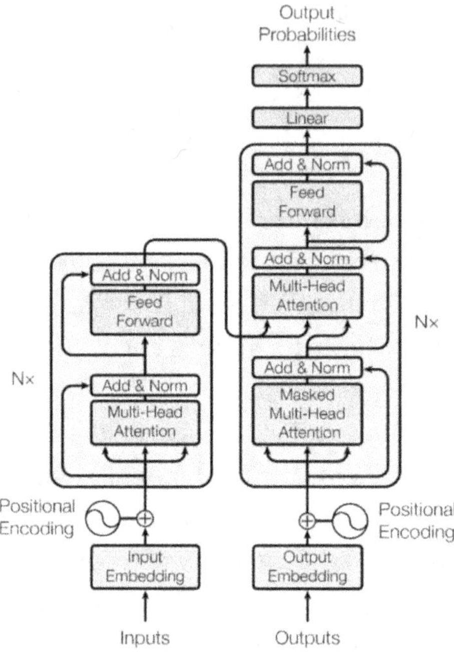

Figure 4-6. *The architecture of the transformer*
Source: "Attention Is All You Need," by Vaswani, et al.

In an RNN, all the hidden states are collected in a vector, which can be defined as a *vector of values*. The decoder creates a *query vector*, which is the result of the decoding.

The attention uses a similar vector, but instead of using all the hidden states, the attention will create a weighted sum of the values in the vector values. The weighted sum depends on the query vector, and in a simple world, for every data point the encoder reads, the attention mechanism takes into consideration another input at the same time. This improves the translation of the input to the output.

As shown in Figure 4-6, the transformer architecture is based on attention layers. In a transformer, the input data can be sent in parallel, and this, combined with the new GPU hardware, allows the hardware to be used effectively and speeds up the training process.

The first step of every transformer is the *input embedding*, whereby the data in the input is embedded and translated into a numerical value. Remember that machine learning algorithms work only with numbers. This layer creates different vectors, with different data in the input.

The following step assigns some positional information to the embedding data. The encoder has no recurrence like the RNN, and to provide better understanding of the data, we need to add the position of the data into the input embeddings. This is done using the *positional encoding*. There are many variants of positional encoding; the transformer uses the sine and cosine functions to calculate the positional encoding.

$$PE_{(pos,2i)} = sin\left(pos / 10000^{2i/d_{model}}\right)$$

$$PE_{(pos,2i+1)} = cos\left(pos / 10000^{2i/d_{model}}\right)$$

Where *pos* is the actual position, *i* is the dimension, and each dimension of the embedding data has a corresponding sine wave.

Immediately after the positional encoding is the *encoding layer*. This layer contains two sub-modules—a *multiheaded attention* and a *fully connected network*. In the case of the decoding part of the network, the decoder has two multiheaded attention layers.

The encoder layer maps all the input sequences into an abstract continuous representation. This representation holds the learned information for the entire sequence. The multiheaded attention applies what is called *self-attention*, which allows the model to associate the input data with the output data. If, for example, the transformer is used for language translation, the multiheaded attention will learn that after the word "there" normally there is the word "is", or it can learn to associate the word "you" after the word "how" and "are". The multiheaded attention has three inputs—K, the key, V, the value vector, and Q, the query. After feeding all three values, the layer will use a dot product on the matrix formed with the three vectors to create a scoring matrix. Then the scores are scaled down, and the result is called *scaled scores*. This is done to avoid the issue of the gradient exploding, one of the issues with RNNs. To scale down the scores, they are divided by the square root of the dimension of the query and the key. This reduces the map.

At this point, you need to isolate the most important value from the lower one. To do that, you calculate the *softmax* of the scaled score. The softmax is used for a simple reason, the value with a high score is heightened, and the one with a lower score is depressed. This allows the model to learn what data is most important. In the case of a model language, this is translated to which words are more likely to be used.

At this point, the output of the multiheaded attention is a vector with scored values. This is added to the original input embedding, called a *residual connection*, and the output formed by the input embedding and the multiheaded attention output vector goes through a layer of normalization.

This normalization layer produces an output, a *normalized residual output*. This output will be processed through a *pointwise feedforward network.*

At this point, the encoding work is done, and the decoding work starts. The goal of the decoder is to generate data based on the input data. As you can see in Figure 4-6, the decoder has a similar layer to the encoding layer. The main difference between the encoding and the decoding is the presence of two multiheaded attentions instead of one, the presence of a pointwise feedforwarded layer, residual connection, and a normalization layer after each sub-layer.

These sub-layers have a similar functionality to the encoder. The only difference is the multiheaded attention layer. The last layer of the decoder is a linear layer and a softmax. The softmax produces the probability to get the correct data based on the input. The decoder works with what is called a *token*. A token is essentially a d-dimensional vector, and in the context of the decoder, the output of the multiheaded attention, the decoder starts to work with the initial token, and as you can see in Figure 4-6. It takes the list of the previous output as inputs and the output of the encoder. This output contains the attention information from the input. The goal of the decoder is to generate a token as an output, and when this is achieved, the job is done.

Latent Variable Models

The family of latent variable generative models learn *latent variables*, which are not observable but are important for defining the data.

Imagine, for example, that you want to create software that reproduces human faces. Faces have a lot of defined variables, such as two eyes, one mouth, and two ears. The generator can start to draw a face with this simple basic information, but is this enough? The simple answer is no.

When we draw an image, this basic information gives us only the silhouette of the actual image. To re-create a clear image, we need to identify the "hidden" factor that makes a human face. For example, the gender, the color of the eyes, and whether they have a beard. All this information makes up the *latent variables*. The goal of the generative model is to identify these variables and learn how to represent them. Examples of generative models that use latent variables is a generative adversarial network (GAN) and variational autoencoders (VAEs).

A Short Introduction to GANs

The generative adversarial network (GAN) was developed by Ian Goodfellow in the paper "Generative Adversarial Nets" in 2014. The basic idea behind GANs is to have two different neural networks that compete against each other. One neural network is the *generator*, the part of the network responsible for the generation of the data. The generator competes against a *discriminator*, and the goal of the discriminator is to classify the data as real or fake. A basic architecture for a GAN is represented in Figure 4-7.

The discriminator starts to generate new data using some noise data, because at the start the generator has no idea how the data looks. The discriminator classifies the data as true or false.

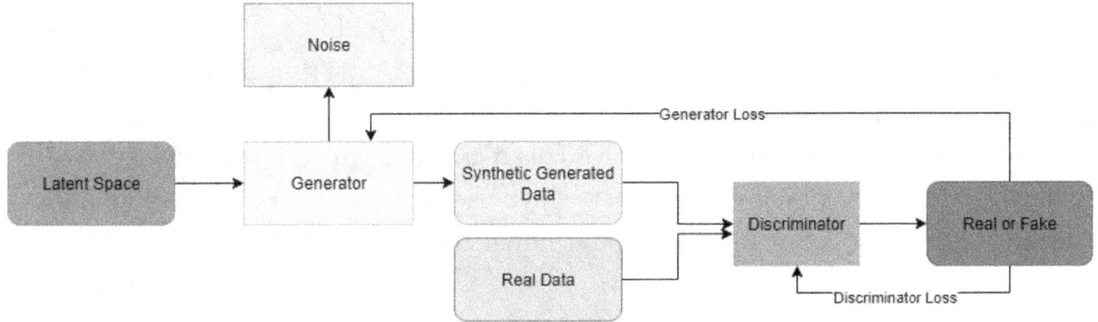

Figure 4-7. *The basic GAN architecture*

The result of the classification produces a *loss* value. This is essentially the error from the classification of the data. The loss value is sent back to adjust the data on the generator and to the discriminator to make it learn how to classify the data better.

This topology of networks is called *adversarial* because the generator and discriminator are trained to compete against each other. The generator tries to generate data that can fool the discriminator, and the discriminator tries to train itself to always recognize the data generated by the generator. To be fully trained, a GAN needs to reach these conditions:

- The *generator* can produce data that is indistinguishable from the real data.

- The *discriminator* cannot distinguish between real or fake data better than 50% of the time.

When both conditions are met, you have a *converged GAN*, which is also called a *Nash Equilibrium*. Training a GAN is like game theory. A GAN is a non-cooperative game, the neural networks compete against each other, and the GAN converge when the generator and the discriminator can no longer improve each other.

This complexity of training a GAN is also a weakness of GANs. The convergence is very complex, requires a lot of time, and is more a condition than a state. When the discriminator can't distinguish the data, it can give a wrong loss to the generator, and this can reduce the quality of the generated data. Nowadays researchers define different techniques for helping GAN training, and you will learn more about this in Chapter 5.

Variational Autoencoders

Another family of generative models that use latent space are variational autoencoders. This architecture was introduced in 2013 by Diedrik and Welling, and similarly to a GAN, it is composed of two distinct parts. The main difference is that they don't compete against each other.

Variational autoencoders are composed of an encoder, which is used to learn and isolate the latent variables, and a decoder, which uses the latent variable to rebuild the data. The basic architecture of a variational autoencoder is shown in Figure 4-8.

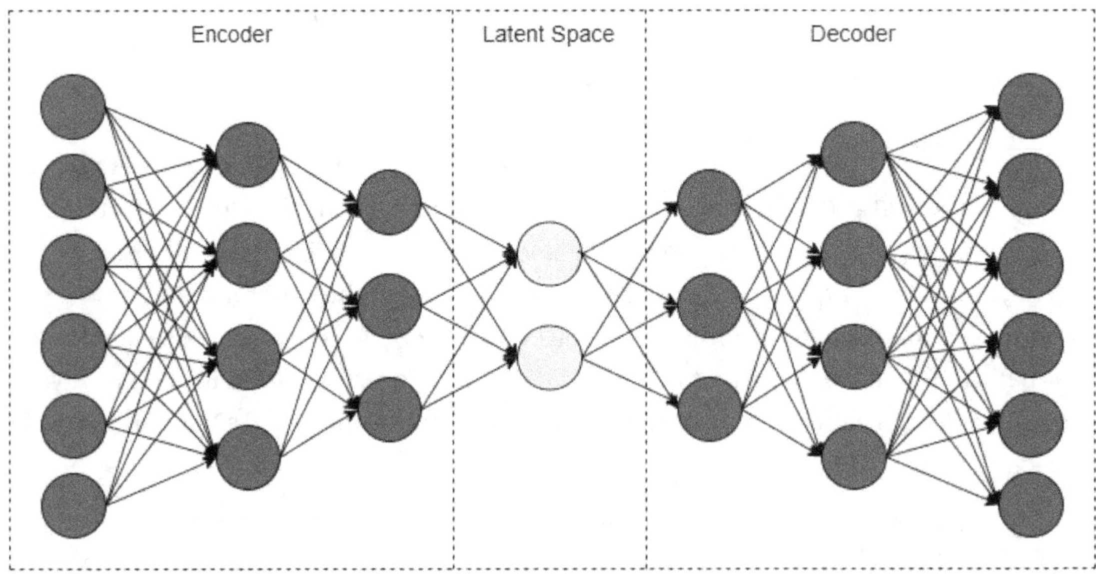

Figure 4-8. *Representation of a variational autoencoder*

The *encoder* part will receive the input data, the data you want to replicate. The encoder will extract the main latent variables from the data. The latent variables serve as the output of the encoder, and they at the same time serve as the input for the decoder. The decoder will use the input from the latent variable to rebuild and re-create the data.

There are similarities between variational autoencoders and the encoder-decoder architecture discussed in the RNN section. Both use an encoding/decoding part. The difference between the two types of architecture is that autoencoders use an unsupervised algorithm, whereas in the architecture analyzed in the RNN, the neural network is aware of the data, and the encoding part is used. Variational autoencoders use ranges from image generation when used in combination with a CNNs, to music and text generation when used in combination with a transformers.

Foundation Models

Foundation models are a new way to classify and identify a model. The name is associated with a specific type of architecture, but they are widely used in the generative modelling space.

The term *foundation model* was defined in 2021 in the paper "On the Opportunities and Risks of Foundation Models." This paper was released by the Center for Research on Foundation Model (CRFM) Stanford Institute for Human-Cantered Artificial Intelligence (HAI) from Stanford University.

The paper defines the foundation model as "Any model that is trained on broad data, generally using self-supervision at scale, that can be adapted, e.g. fine-tuned, to a wide range of downstream tasks". Examples of this model are BERT, GPT-4, and CLIP.

From a technical perspective, the foundation models cover a wide range of tasks, like question answering, sentiment analysis, information extraction, image captioning, object recognition, and instruction following. A foundation model is a type of generative model. In this type of model, you can identify more than one architecture, for example, transformers, GANs, and variational autoencoders can coexist in the same model. The goal is to create output based on different sources.

With foundation models, you centralize the information from different sources, for example, speech, images, text, and structured data. The model will be trained and then used to produce the different types of output.

From an AI perspective, foundation models are important due to *emergence* and *homogenization*. These two words essentially represent all the research around AI. *Emergence* refers to identifying and describing the behavior of a system. In particular, emergence is used to describe that the behavior of a system is implicitly induced rather than explicitly constructed. In other words, the system understands how to act based on some mathematical algorithm. A deep learning algorithm will learn by itself the important features that allow it to classify an object.

Homogenization is a direct consequence of the emergence and is defined as the consolidation of methodologies used to build a machine learning system. This is used to define a wide range of algorithms but will create a single point of failure. For example, the deep learning architecture is a homogenization from where we can specialize different types of tasks, for example, the CNNs for a computer vision task, or the NLPs for a language task.

The processes of emergence and homogenization were born with the history of AI. Scientists defined an algorithm that could identify the "how" behind the data, with the algorithm defined they have the *emergence*, a system that can learn how to execute the task automatically without being specifically programmed for it.

The next step was to homogenize the algorithm used to learn the data. In this context, algorithms like linear regression are defined, which solve the second problem, and have a common algorithm that can be used for learning.

At this point, we have the foundation algorithm that can be used to learn the "how" behind the data, but why is it so important to define the foundation model? Recall from Chapter 1 the definition of artificial intelligence:

> *The science and engineering of making computer machines able to perform a task that normally requires human intelligence.*

This definition can be used to explain the importance of foundation models, because the final goal of artificial intelligence is to build a system that can emulate human intelligence. This means that a model or an architecture can't just execute one task; it needs to have the ability to execute different types of task. Human intelligence is wider than we can we emulate. For example, consider the theory of multiple intelligence defined by Howard Gardner. In his study, Gardner defines eight types of intelligence:

- *Linguistic*, which is the ability to analyze information and create products involving oral and writing language.

- *Logical-mathematical*, which is the ability to develop equations and proofs, make calculations, and solve abstract problems.

- *Spatial,* which is the ability to recognize and manipulate large-scale and fine-grained spatial images.

- *Musical,* which is the ability to produce, remember, and make meaning of different patterns of sound.

- *Naturalist,* which is the ability to identify and distinguish among different types of plants, animals, and weather formations that are found in the animal world.

- *Bodily-kinesthetics,* which is the ability to use one's own body to create products or solve a problem.

- *Interpersonal,* which is the ability to recognize and understand other people's moods, desires, motivations, and intentions.

- *Intrapersonal,* which is the ability to recognize and understand one's moods, desires, motivations, and intentions.

The subsequent studies identify that every human has all these types of intelligence, and each has a different strength. No two individuals, not even identical twins, exhibit precisely the same profile of intelligence strengths and weaknesses.

In this sense, the development of foundation models is a mandatory step for the evolution of AI, in particular, if we want to achieve artificial general intelligence, AGI.

At the moment, the foundation models are strictly connected to the generative model, in particular with LLMs. This is mainly because the definition is quite new and was essentially made after the release of models like GPT-3, CLIP, and other similar models. These models are at the moment under research and there is a lack of understanding of the risks and potential of them. Understanding what these models are is important, particularly if you want to build a career in the area of generative models.

Conclusion

This chapter covered generative artificial intelligence. It defined the theoretical basics and some of the uses for the main architecture. It also introduced the transformer. Transformers are important changes in the area of AI and were initially used for language tasks. They became popular and the basis of many foundation models, including GPT (Generative Pretrained Transformer).

Nowadays transformers are not only used for language tasks but for any task that works with recursive data. For example, the vision transformer is used for image classification and a transformer-like architecture.

Another important topic touched on was the foundation model. This type of model is not connected to a specific generative model architecture, but is strictly connected to the deep generative model. Foundation models are probably the next important step in AI and take another step toward the realization of artificial general intelligence.

The Stanford study about foundation models shows how important these models are, but at the same time e the risks connected with these models. Foundation models are very important if we want to make another step in the direction of AGI because human intelligence can't be classified as just one single type. There are at least eight different types of intelligence. The foundation models must be able to use all the eight types of intelligence.

The next chapter helps you begin to develop a generative model. You'll start with GANs. This architecture is mainly used to generate new images, and the misuse of this architecture creates what is now known as a *deepfake*. GANs were developed by Ian Goodfellow in 2014, and in the ensuing years they have gained popularity. In the next chapter, you use Julia and Python to develop a GAN.

## CHAPTER 5

Generative Adversarial Networks (GANs)

The first architecture we explore is *Generative Adversarial Networks* (GANs). This type of architecture is widely used to generate new images. This architecture was introduced in 2014 by Ian Goodfellow, and since then it has grown in popularity. What makes GANs interesting is their capacity to produce data that is similar but not equal to the original data. The synthetic data generated is incredibly realistic, which makes GANs the ideal architecture for a wide range of uses. The best is when GANs are used to generate new images. This chapter explores GANs and shows you how to write your own GANs using Python and Julia.

Basic GAN Architecture

Before you start to develop your first GANs, is important to understand the basic architecture of the GANs, and how this specific type of network is developed and trained. As you know from Chapter 4, GANs are composed of two neural network architectures that compete against each other.

The first component of GANs is called the *generator*, and the goal of this component is to generate synthetic data that approximates the real data distributions. The second component of the GANs is called the *discriminator*, and the goal of this component is to classify the synthetic data as false.

These components compete against each other because the generator tries to create data that can fool the discriminator and the discriminator tries not to be fooled by the generator. This type of training is called *adversarial training,* and this is where the architecture gets the name. The basic architecture of a GAN is shown in Figure 5-1. The next section describes the different GAN components and explains how they are used to generate new data.

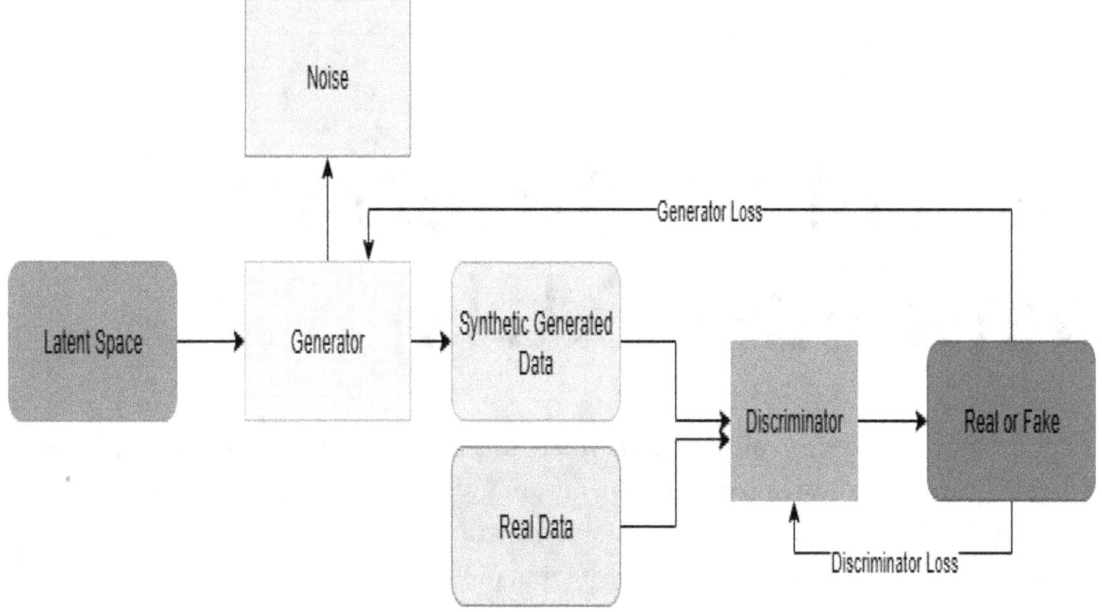

Figure 5-1. *The basic GAN architecture*

The loss of the GANs is calculated as a two players—*MinMax Loss*. The formula to calculate the MinMax Loss is the following:

$$\min_{G}\max_{D} V(D,G) = E_{x \sim p_{dt}(x)}\big[logD(x)\big] + Ez \sim p_{z(z)}\big[log\big(1 - D\big(G(z)\big)\big)\big]$$

Where:

- G is the generator and D is the discriminator

- The sample data p_{datax} is indicated by x

- The random noise $p_x(z)$ is indicated by z

- D(x) is the discriminator likelihood of correctly identifying real data

- D(G(z)) is the discriminator likelihood of identifying generated data as real

The value of the function is calculated as a sum of the loss function, which is used to train the discriminator and the generator.

The Generator

The *generator* is the core component of the GANs, and the goal of a generator is to generate synthetic data that is *similar* to the original data. This an important note to keep in mind—the GAN produces data that is similar but not the same as the original, and this capability allows the GANs to be used in areas where privacy is important because the synthetic data can be used to avoid potential privacy issues.

At the start, the generator takes random noise and uses it as a starting point to generate new data. The data is sent to the discriminator for evaluation, and the result is the loss of the data, which is sent back to the generator. It will be used to generate a new set of data, starting from the noisy one. The generator will continue to improve the data generated until the discriminator is no longer able to distinguish between the real and synthetic data. See Listing 5-1.

Listing 5-1. A Code Example of a GAN Generator

```python
def make_generator_model():
    model = tf.keras.Sequential()

    model.add(layers.Dense(7 * 7 * 256, use_bias=False, input_
    shape=(100,)))
    model.add(layers.BatchNormalization())
    model.add(layers.LeakyReLU())

    model.add(layers.Reshape((7, 7, 256)))

    model.add(layers.Conv2DTranspose(128, (5, 5), strides=(1, 1),
    padding='same', use_bias=False))
    model.add(layers.BatchNormalization())
    model.add(layers.LeakyReLU())

    model.add(layers.Conv2DTranspose(64, (5, 5), strides=(2, 2),
    padding='same', use_bias=False))
    model.add(layers.BatchNormalization())
    model.add(layers.LeakyReLU())

    model.add(layers.Conv2DTranspose(1, (5, 5), strides=(2, 2),
    padding='same', use_bias=False, activation='tanh'))

    return model
```

The Discriminator

The *discriminator* is responsible for the classification of the data as real or false. At its core, a discriminator is a binary classifier that distinguishes the data.

The discriminator plays a vital role in the quality of the data generated by the GANs, because the result of its classification is sent back to the generator, and it is used to improve the quality of the generated data. At the start, the generator will receive data from the real dataset and the generated one and try to classify them correctly. The training of the discriminator will impact the general quality of the GANs because a bad discriminator can classify very noisy data as real, which reduces the quality of the data that's generated. See Listing 5-2.

Listing 5-2. Code Examples of a Discriminator

```
def make_discriminator_model():
    model = tf.keras.Sequential()

    model.add(layers.Conv2D(64, (5, 5), strides=(2, 2), padding='same',
    input_shape=[28, 28, 1]))
    model.add(layers.LeakyReLU())
    model.add(layers.Dropout(0.3))

    model.add(layers.Conv2D(128, (5, 5), strides=(2, 2), padding='same'))
    model.add(layers.LeakyReLU())
    model.add(layers.Dropout(0.3))

    model.add(layers.Flatten())
    model.add(layers.Dense(1))

    return model
```

Training a GAN

As mentioned, a GAN is an adversarial network whose basic architecture consists of two neural networks competing against each other. The discriminator's goal is to identify whether the data is fake or real, whereas the generator's goal is to create data that is similar to the real data.

This type of training is a *zero-sum game*, which means that the gain for the generator means the discriminator has lost the capacity to identify whether the data is real or fake. This type of training is what makes GANs so effective, and at the same time, it can raise some potential issues during training.

The first problem is connected to the generator itself. This type of problem is called the *mode collapse phenomenon*, and it happens when the generator produces the same output for multiple interactions. This leads the discriminator to recognize only that specific set of data as fake. The GANs will therefore produce very low-quality images.

Another common issue of this type of training are *vanishing gradients*. In this case, the discriminator is nearly perfect in the identification of the fake data, which makes it difficult for the generator to produce data that can fool the discriminator, and this can make it difficult produce output.

Another problem of GANs and adversarial training is *instability*. For correct training, you need to train the generator and the discriminator at the same time. This means that the result of the one can impact and influence the outcome of the other.

Researchers develop different methodologies to address these problems. Some of them have introduced regularizations in terms of the loss function, which help the generator produce a wider range of examples. This wider range of examples helps produce better quality data. Some other researchers propose a new architecture for the generator and the discriminator. Examples of this new architecture are the Wasserstein GANs and CycleGANs. Some other researchers explored the usage of multiple discriminators, which can provide more detailed feedback to the generator and then to improve the quality of the data generated.

GAN Flavors

GANs can show some problems during the training phase and this can impact the quality of the data produced by a GAN. Researchers have developed different methodologies and architectures for GANs—let's briefly look at these different techniques.

The first variation is called *Conditional Generative Adversarial Network*, CGAN. This variation can generate data based on specific conditions. The condition can be, for example, the class labels of the data. This type of GAN changes the way the GANs are trained, and the conditional GAN changes the architecture of the GAN. Figure 5-2 shows this new architecture. As you can see, the labels are used to indicate the type of data ingested in the networks.

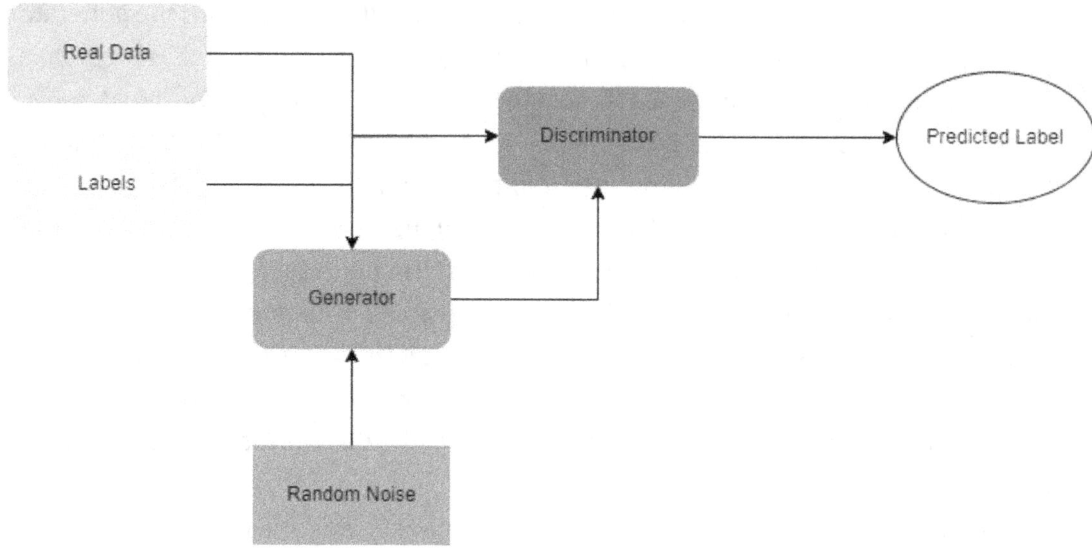

Figure 5-2. *The conditional GAN architectural diagram*

In the CGAN, the generator and the discriminator both receive the label for the data to be generated. This technique allows the GAN to generate a specific type of data, allowing it to be more exact in the generation.

In 2017, NVIDIA introduced the paper "Progressive Growing of GANs for Improved Quality, Stability, and Variation," which presented what is called ProGANs. They do not change the architecture of the GANs like conditional GANs, but change the way GANs are trained. The core principle behind ProGANs is to train the GAN starting with a small image and then add layers with bigger images. This helps the GANs create more realistic images. Figure 5-3 shows the layer for the ProGAN.

Another improvement in training GANs is with Wasserstein GANs, WGAN, which was introduced in 2017, and the WGAN was introduced to solve the problem of the convergence of the GANs. The difference between the GAN and WGAN is the use of a different loss function. This new loss function uses the Wasserstein distance to calculate the distance between the two probability distributions of the generator, and the probability distribution of the real images. The goal of WGAN is to enhance the stability of the training and allow the GAN to avoid the issue of the training instability.

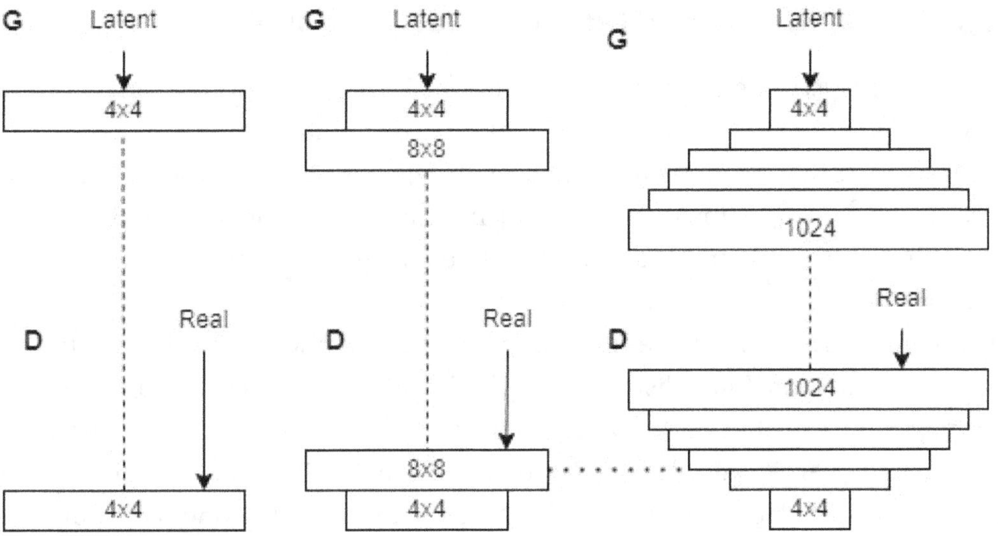

Figure 5-3. *The layer of the ProGAN*

Evaluating the Result of GANs

Evaluating the result of a GAN can be tricky because you need to evaluate the result of
the generated data. The generative models can be evaluated in the same way they are in
supervised learning algorithms, because you don't have a basic ground to check the real
data. Because of that, metrics like F1-score and accuracy can't give a perfect evaluation
of the GANs. You will see later why, and because of that, different methods are created
that help evaluate the GANs. These methods are as follows:

- *Inception score* measures the balance between the quality and the
  diversity of the generated sample.

- *Frechet inception distance* calculates the distance between the
  distribution of real and generated data in a feature space.

One of the major uses of GANs is with image generation. One of the most commonly
used evaluation techniques is *visual inspection*. This technique allows for a faster visual
check, but of course, this is not the best if you want to measure the quality of the data.
Another problem is the number of images that can be visually inspected. This type of
inspection is valid only when you have a short number of images. If you want to improve
the quality, you can use the other two metrics (the inception score and the fréchet
inception distance).

Inception Score and Fréchet Inception Distance

The most widely used metric is the *inception score*, IS. It is used to evaluate the effectiveness of a GAN, and in particular, measures the quality of the generated images.

The basic idea is that good quality images should have a good variety of different and realistic images. The images should look like the images from the training set. To compute the inception score, you use a pretrained image classification model called the *InceptionV3 model*.

The generated images will be sent as input to the InceptionV3 model, and the output will be the probability distribution over the different objects that are present in the image. The distribution will be then compared to the uniform distribution, and the Kullback-Leibler (KL) divergence between the two distributions is measured. One distribution is the output of the InceptionV3 model and the other one is the output of the GAN.

The Kullback-Leibler divergence is a statistical measure of the distance between two probability distributions, P and Q. This is denoted as $D_{KL}(P \parallel Q)$ and is used to ensure that the new image doesn't drastically deviate from the training image. In a simple world, the KL ensures that the generated images are similar to the original ones, which ensures that the quality of the images is always as high as possible. The possible value from the KL can take a value from 0 to infinite.

The result of the Kullback-Leibler divergence indicates how "near" the images are to the real ones. If the distance is small, the images are both different and of good quality. If the result of the distance is large, the images are of low quality and not variable enough.

The Fréchet Inception Distance, FID, was introduced in 2017. The FID measures the distance between the two images, where the IS uses only the generated image. The FID use a pretrained model, for example, the InceptionV3 model, and calculates the statistical distance between the value of the generated image and the real image. The FID is essentially an improvement of the IS score because it uses two images to calculate the value.

Using Precision and Recall to Evaluate a GAN

Precision, recall, and F1 can be used to evaluate the final work of GANs. For example, precision can be used to measure how much of the generated sample data is classified as real. Recall measures how much real sample data can be generated by the GAN.

The problem with the GAN-generated data is determining what is "real" data in a high dimensional space. This issue can be addressed using nearest-neighbor matching, which involves finding the closest real sample to each generated sample in the feature space. When this is done in a pretrained model, the similarity is compared. The generated data with major similarity is considered real.

Limitations of GAN Metrics

The metrics mentioned earlier can be used to evaluate some aspects of a GAN but they all have limitations. The FID and the IS mainly use the InceptionV3 model, which is trained using the ImageNet dataset. If you try to evaluate the network with an image that's not present in that dataset, the metrics can be incorrect.

To solve this problem, you can try to use other metrics like recall and precision to evaluate the GANs, but these metrics can also have problems, particularly after a human visual inspection of the result. The solution to this problem is always good judgment. Because of the nature of the GAN itself, these types of models are mainly used to produce images. Human review remains a valid alternative.

GAN Use Cases

Before you start writing some code, it's important to review some potential GAN use cases. GANs are primarily used to manipulate images, which covers different areas of image manipulation, including:

- **Image synthesis:** The GAN creates a completely new image never generated before. The image is similar to the real one but not the same.

- **Super-resolution:** The GAN is used to improve the quality of the image. The GAN is trained with high-resolution images, and then applied to low-resolution images. Because of the capabilities of the GAN to learn latent variables, the GAN will improve the quality of the original images.

- **Data argumentation:** GANs can create similar data, which can be used to improve the quality of the data. This is particularly useful when collecting quality data is expensive, such as in the medical field, environmental studies, and in all of the areas where there is not enough data.

- **Entertainment industry:** GANs can be used in the entertainment industry to create animations for film or music production.

- **Time series:** GANs can generate missing time series information, which can be useful in finance or any application of the time series.

- **Art:** MIT introduced the project GAN Paint Studio, where GANs are used to generate painting scenes.

- **Anomaly detection:** GANs are employed in the area of anomaly detection. One of the uses is f-AnoGAN, which identifies any anomalies in images.

The following example is just one example of a GAN use case. Because of their nature, GANs have a lot of potential in different areas. The goal of the book is not to show you all the GAN use cases, but to give you the tools to build your own GANs. Let's then start to write your first GAN, a vanilla GAN, using Julia and Python. For this experiment, you will use the MINST dataset.

Your First Vanilla GAN

This first approach is a vanilla GAN and this type of network is the simplest. The dataset used is the MINST, because it is the most used and known.

First you need to define some imports and some general values used in the code (see Listing 5-3). You can download the full code from the book's repo.

Listing 5-3. The imports and variables Used in the Code

```
import tensorflow as tf
from tensorflow.keras import layers
import numpy as np
import matplotlib.pyplot as plt
```

```python
# Load the MNIST dataset
(train_images, _), (_, _) = tf.keras.datasets.mnist.load_data()

# Normalize the images to [-1, 1] (this helps with the training stability)
train_images = train_images.reshape(train_images.shape[0], 28, 28,
1).astype('float32')
train_images = (train_images - 127.5) / 127.5  # Rescale images to [-1, 1]

# Define constants
BUFFER_SIZE = 60000
BATCH_SIZE = 256
NOISE_DIM = 100  # Dimension of the noise vector (latent space)

# Create the dataset
train_dataset = tf.data.Dataset.from_tensor_slices(train_images).
shuffle(BUFFER_SIZE).batch(BATCH_SIZE)
```

A GAN is composed of two main parts, the generator and the discriminator.
Listing 5-4 shows the implementation of the generator using Python.

Listing 5-4. The Python Implementation of the Generator Code

```python
def make_generator_model():
    model = tf.keras.Sequential()

    # Dense layer to upscale the noise input
    model.add(layers.Dense(7 * 7 * 256, use_bias=False, input_
    shape=(NOISE_DIM,)))
    model.add(layers.BatchNormalization())
    model.add(layers.LeakyReLU())

    # Reshape the output into a 7x7x256 feature map
    model.add(layers.Reshape((7, 7, 256)))

    # First transposed convolution layer (upsampling)
    model.add(layers.Conv2DTranspose(128, (5, 5), strides=(1, 1),
    padding='same', use_bias=False))
    model.add(layers.BatchNormalization())
    model.add(layers.LeakyReLU())
```

```python
# Second transposed convolution layer (upsampling)
model.add(layers.Conv2DTranspose(64, (5, 5), strides=(2, 2),
padding='same', use_bias=False))
model.add(layers.BatchNormalization())
model.add(layers.LeakyReLU())

# Third transposed convolution layer to output a 28x28x1 image
model.add(layers.Conv2DTranspose(1, (5, 5), strides=(2, 2),
padding='same', use_bias=False, activation='tanh'))

return model
```

The generator starts with a *dense* layer, also called a *fully-connected layer*. This type of layer is used to create an abstract representation of the input data. In this layer, every neuron is connected to every neuron in the preceding layer.

This layer transforms the input noise, and the GAN transforms the noise in the specific data into a feature map—in particular, the dense layer creates a feature map of 7x7x256.

The next layer is the *Batch Normalization* layer, which normalizes the input data to maintain the mean output close to 0 and the output standard deviation close to 1. Batch normalization is very important when you train an artificial neural network, because it helps the network be stable and faster. At this point, you have the first basic neural network, and you have normalized the input. Now you need an activation function. This example uses *Leaky ReLU*.

The *Leaky Rectified Linear Unit* or Leaky ReLU is a type of activation function based on the ReLU but the main difference is a small slope for negative values instead of a flat slope. This type of activation function is used when a task can suffer from sparse gradient, and for this reason, it has become popular across the generative adversarial network.

At this point, you add a *reshape* layer, which reshapes the data and ensures that it is in the dimension you need for the next steps. This is important because for the next processing, you need to be sure about the dimension of the data.

The next layers are very important for a GAN. These layers start with a *transposed convolutional layer*, which is essentially the opposite of a convolutional layer. The goal of a transposed layer is to get the input data and "generate" a new image. This process is used to create the data and "expand" it to have a final image. After the transposed convolution, you a fully connected layer and an activation layer apply another time; this process is repeated three times. The last time, as you can see from the code, we changed the activation function by adding a *tahn*. Because we finished the model, we didn't add another layer, so the usage of the tahn is because the result of the activation is between -1 and 1. This is useful when you need to have different shades of colors. The result of all the upsampling is an image with a size of 28x28, the same size as a MINST image.

Important note: The model we use is *sequential*, which means that all the layers are stacked one after the other in a sequence. Figure 5-4 shows the result of this model, as well as the number of trainable parameters.

```
Model: "sequential"
```

Layer (type)	Output Shape	Param #
dense (Dense)	(None, 12544)	1,254,400
batch_normalization (BatchNormalization)	(None, 12544)	50,176
leaky_re_lu (LeakyReLU)	(None, 12544)	0
reshape (Reshape)	(None, 7, 7, 256)	0
conv2d_transpose (Conv2DTranspose)	(None, 7, 7, 128)	819,200
batch_normalization_1 (BatchNormalization)	(None, 7, 7, 128)	512
leaky_re_lu_1 (LeakyReLU)	(None, 7, 7, 128)	0
conv2d_transpose_1 (Conv2DTranspose)	(None, 14, 14, 64)	204,800
batch_normalization_2 (BatchNormalization)	(None, 14, 14, 64)	256
leaky_re_lu_2 (LeakyReLU)	(None, 14, 14, 64)	0
conv2d_transpose_2 (Conv2DTranspose)	(None, 28, 28, 1)	1,600

```
Total params: 2,330,944 (8.89 MB)
Trainable params: 2,305,472 (8.79 MB)
Non-trainable params: 25,472 (99.50 KB)
```

Figure 5-4. *The model created for the GAN in the vanilla GAN*

The next important component of the vanilla GAN is the *discriminator*. Listing 5-5 shows the discriminator.

Listing 5-5. The Code for the Discriminator

```python
def make_discriminator_model():
    model = tf.keras.Sequential()

    # First convolutional layer
    model.add(layers.Conv2D(64, (5, 5), strides=(2, 2), padding='same',
    input_shape=[28, 28, 1]))
    model.add(layers.LeakyReLU())
    model.add(layers.Dropout(0.3))

    # Second convolutional layer
    model.add(layers.Conv2D(128, (5, 5), strides=(2, 2), padding='same'))
    model.add(layers.LeakyReLU())
    model.add(layers.Dropout(0.3))

    # Classify the image
    model.add(layers.Flatten())
    model.add(layers.Dense(1))

    return model
```

The discriminator is a simple CNN and the goal of the discriminator is to classify an image as real or fake. That is why the best choice is a CNN.

The CNN use the convolutional layer, which is used to reduce the dimension of the image. This is the opposite of the transposed layer used in the generator. In this architecture we use a *dropout* layer, which prevents overfitting. The last components of the CNN are the *flatten* layer and the *dense* layer, which are used to classify the image as real or fake.

The flatten layer reduces the dimensionality of the data before passing it to a fully connected layer, in this case, the dense layer. The dense layer will return a value between 0 and 1, indicating whether the image is fake or real. Figure 5-5 shows the discriminator created with this code.

```
Model: "sequential_1"
```

Layer (type)	Output Shape	Param #
conv2d (Conv2D)	(None, 14, 14, 64)	1,664
leaky_re_lu_3 (LeakyReLU)	(None, 14, 14, 64)	0
dropout (Dropout)	(None, 14, 14, 64)	0
conv2d_1 (Conv2D)	(None, 7, 7, 128)	204,928
leaky_re_lu_4 (LeakyReLU)	(None, 7, 7, 128)	0
dropout_1 (Dropout)	(None, 7, 7, 128)	0
flatten (Flatten)	(None, 6272)	0
dense_1 (Dense)	(None, 1)	6,273

```
Total params: 212,865 (831.50 KB)
Trainable params: 212,865 (831.50 KB)
Non-trainable params: 0 (0.00 B)
```

Figure 5-5. *The discriminator model created by the code for the vanilla GANs*

Loss Calculations

Another important component of the GANs is the calculation of *loss*. GANs have two different neural networks that compete against each other, and the loss calculated by the discriminator is used to adjust the discriminator and the generator.

In this example, we use one of the probabilistic loss functions, BinaryCrossentropy. The loss function is very important when you need to understand how the generative artificial networks work. A loss function calculates and represents the price paid for the inaccuracy of a prediction.

In the classification problem, like the one the discriminator needs to achieve, the loss function calculates the best prediction for the label y giving a function $f: X \rightarrow y$. In our case, the loss function gives the best result for the classification as real or fake. In the code, we use Binary Cross Entropy, as shown in Listing 5-6.

Listing 5-6. The Code for Calculating the BinaryCrossentropy

```
# Define the loss and optimizers
cross_entropy = tf.keras.losses.BinaryCrossentropy(from_logits=True)

def discriminator_loss(real_output, fake_output):
```

```
    real_loss = cross_entropy(tf.ones_like(real_output), real_output)
    fake_loss = cross_entropy(tf.zeros_like(fake_output), fake_output)
    total_loss = real_loss + fake_loss
    return total_loss

def generator_loss(fake_output):
    return cross_entropy(tf.ones_like(fake_output), fake_output)
```

Binary Cross Entropy is a loss function that measures the difference between the actual predicted binary outcome and the real binary labels. The function quantifies how dissimilar the data is, using the real data and the fake data. The loss calculated is used to calculate the total loss of the discriminator and then to update the value for the discriminator. This value will be used during the training phase, as explained in the next section.

Training the GANs

Training the GANs is a two-component task—the discriminator tries to identify if the data are real of fake, and the generator tries to fool the discriminator. The code for managing the training process is shown in Listing 5-7.

Listing 5-7. The Code for Training the GANs

```
@tf.function
def train_step(images):
    noise = tf.random.normal([BATCH_SIZE, NOISE_DIM])

    with tf.GradientTape() as gen_tape, tf.GradientTape() as disc_tape:
        generated_images = generator(noise, training=True)

        real_output = discriminator(images, training=True)
        fake_output = discriminator(generated_images, training=True)

        gen_loss = generator_loss(fake_output)
        disc_loss = discriminator_loss(real_output, fake_output)

    gradients_of_generator = gen_tape.gradient(gen_loss, generator.
    trainable_variables)
```

```python
    gradients_of_discriminator = disc_tape.gradient(disc_loss,
    discriminator.trainable_variables)

    generator_optimizer.apply_gradients(zip(gradients_of_generator,
    generator.trainable_variables))
    discriminator_optimizer.apply_gradients(zip(gradients_of_discriminator,
    discriminator.trainable_variables))

def train(dataset, epochs):
    for epoch in range(epochs):
        for image_batch in dataset:
            train_step(image_batch)

        generate_and_save_images(generator, epoch + 1, seed)

    # Generate after the final epoch
    generate_and_save_images(generator, epochs, seed)

# Generate and save images function
def generate_and_save_images(model, epoch, test_input):
    predictions = model(test_input, training=False)

    fig = plt.figure(figsize=(4, 4))

    for i in range(predictions.shape[0]):
        plt.subplot(4, 4, i+1)
        plt.imshow(predictions[i, :, :, 0] * 127.5 + 127.5, cmap='gray')
        plt.axis('off')

    print('Saved image for epoch {}'.format(epoch))
    plt.show()

# Train the model
train(train_dataset, EPOCHS)
```

Let's explore the code and see how the training works. The starting point of the training is the code in the line train(train_dataset, EPOCHS). This code has variables, which are an important part of the training process. The first is train_dataset and the other is the epochs. The training dataset is essentially a part of the dataset used to train the model. When you train a machine learning model or artificial intelligence, the dataset is normally split into two groups—the training dataset and the test dataset. If you want to improve this, you can split the data into three datasets, as follows:

- Train dataset, which normally contains between 60% and 80% of the data

- Test dataset, which normally contains between 10% and 20% of the data

- Validation dataset, which normally contains between 10% and 20% of the data

Splitting the data into different datasets helps train and evaluate the model. When you create the dataset, it is better to get some random data, because you can then cover all the different types of data and avoid overfitting or underfitting problems from the data. In this case, we use the MINST dataset, which is split into two different datasets, Train and Test. In our case, the Train dataset size is 60,000 and the Test dataset size is 10,000 elements. The other important variable for the training process is the *epochs*.

The epoch is the number of times the model will go through the elements in the dataset; it is also the number of iterations of all the training data in one cycle. This is an important value when you train your model. An epoch is defined as a *hyperparameter*.

Because there is no sense and the algorithm didn't learn something to go through all the data more than one time, with the epoch there is another hyperparameter, called the *batch size*. You essentially define how many elements of the training set are present in every epoch. In this code, the epoch is 100 and the batch size is 256. The starting point is the `train` function, which is quite simple:

```
def train(dataset, epochs):
    for epoch in range(epochs):
        for image_batch in dataset:
            train_step(image_batch)

        generate_and_save_images(generator, epoch + 1, seed)

    # Generate after the final epoch
    generate_and_save_images(generator, epochs, seed)
```

The code uses a simple for loop, for epoch in range(epochs). Inside the first loop is a nested loop. It contains a subset of the image from the dataset, for image_batch in dataset, and with this subset, it calls the train_step function. The train_step function is essentially the core of the training process:

```
@tf.function
def train_step(images):
    noise = tf.random.normal([BATCH_SIZE, NOISE_DIM])

    with tf.GradientTape() as gen_tape, tf.GradientTape() as disc_tape:
        generated_images = generator(noise, training=True)

        real_output = discriminator(images, training=True)
        fake_output = discriminator(generated_images, training=True)

        gen_loss = generator_loss(fake_output)
        disc_loss = discriminator_loss(real_output, fake_output)

    gradients_of_generator = gen_tape.gradient(gen_loss, generator.
    trainable_variables)
    gradients_of_discriminator = disc_tape.gradient(disc_loss,
    discriminator.trainable_variables)

    generator_optimizer.apply_gradients(zip(gradients_of_generator,
    generator.trainable_variables))
    discriminator_optimizer.apply_gradients(zip(gradients_of_discriminator,
    discriminator.trainable_variables))
```

This function introduces a very interesting Python functionality called a *decorator*, which is Python syntax that changes the behavior of the function itself. In this case, the decorator is @tf.function. This decorator optimizes the code and transforms the Python function into graph operations, which speeds up the execution process.

The function starts with noise generation because as we know the first image created by a GAN is simple noise. The next step is to generate an image:

```
    with tf.GradientTape() as gen_tape, tf.GradientTape() as disc_tape:
        generated_images = generator(noise, training=True)

        real_output = discriminator(images, training=True)
        fake_output = discriminator(generated_images, training=True)
```

```
gen_loss = generator_loss(fake_output)
disc_loss = discriminator_loss(real_output, fake_output)
```

In this code, we see another interesting functionality for TensorFlow. The `tf.GradientTape()` is a specific functionality of TensorFlow.

This specific functionality is used to implement the *automatic differentiation,* which is a set of mathematical techniques that calculate the partial derivative of a function. This technique is very important in the field of machine learning. One of its applications, for example, allows it to implement the backpropagation in a neural network. The `GradientTape()`, in TensorFlow, is an API that provides automatic differentiation; it is used to calculate the gradient. The `with` statement is simply used to manage the generation of the image based on the gradient. In the block, you can see how the code creates the different images.

The first image is based only on the noise, and then the code will calculate the loss function for the generated data. The loss is important because gives the generator and the discriminator the distance between the two images. The longer the distance, the bigger the difference between the two images. Immediately after the `with`, you can see how the code will calculate the gradient; this evaluates the model and determines what adjustments are needed. The training will continue based on the epoch and if all the code is okay, you will see something like Figure 5-6. You can clearly see that the GANs start to generate an image similar to a number, starting only from a bunch of points.

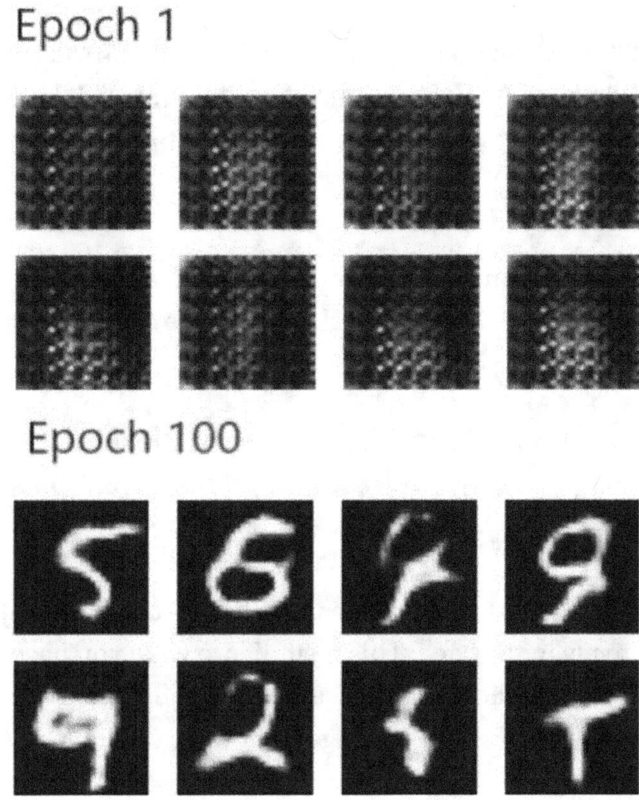

Figure 5-6. The image generated by the GANs. On top you can see how the image improved starting from 1 epoch to 100

As you can see, GANs have the capability to start with a simple set of images and produce data similar to the original data. All they do is start with simple noise and use adversarial training to improve until they reach a final result. I suggest you play with the hyperparameter, the epoch, and the batch and see how this can change the result of your vanilla GAN. In the meantime, let's implement the same GANs, this time using Julia.

Implementing a Vanilla GAN with Julia

It is now time to implement a vanilla GAN using Julia. One of the main differences that Julia has with Python is its extremely compact code.

Julia doesn't have a full integration with TensorFlow. In this case, we use other libraries that achieve the same goal. The library is called *Flux*, and because we need to have the MSIT data, we will install another package. Install the *Flux, MLDatasets, CUDA,* and *Images* packages.

If you are using Colab, you need to install Julia. The repo provides the full Colab with the Julia installation. The Colab is based on the official Julia one. You can use Flux instead, if you want to use the local Julia installation and an Anaconda environment or pure Julia.

Install the package in Julia using the built-in package manager, Pkg. You can do that directly in the code. In my case, I use a Google Colab. The code for installing the package is shown in Listing 5-8.

Listing 5-8. The Code for Installing the Necessary Julia Package

```
using Pkg
Pkg.add(["Flux", "MLDatasets", "CUDA", "Images"])
```

Installing packages in Julia is easier than in Python because Julia allows you to use its package manager directly in the code. This is similar to what you have in Go, and this can reduce the complexity of the package management for the software. When you install the package, you will see the list of all the packages that will be installed or updated in Julia, something like this:

```
151 dependencies successfully precompiled in 536 seconds. 128 already
precompiled.
6 dependencies precompiled but different versions are currently loaded.
Restart julia to access the new versions
```

With the package installed, you can start to write code. In order to understand the main differences between Julia and Python, let's first explore how to create the two main components of the GAN in Julia. The first piece of code to analyze is the generator; the code is presented in Listing 5-9.

Listing 5-9. The Code for the Generator Network in Julia

```
function build_generator()
    print("Build the Generator")
    Chain(
        Dense(100, 256, relu),
        BatchNorm(256),
```

```
    Dense(256, 512, relu),
    BatchNorm(512),
    Dense(512, 784, tanh)
end
```

The Julia code is much more compact than the Python code, because of the framework we use and because Julia is specifically designed to be used in this specific field. The role of the generator is to create a synthetic image. Similar to what we have done with Python, the neural network we develop is based on stacks of layers. In Julia we can do that using the `Chain()` function. The parameters of the function are essentially the layers you want to stack on the neural network. The function essentially connects the output of the previous layer to the input of the other layer.

The first layer of the chain of layers is the *densely connected layer*, or the *fully connected layer*, which is created with the `Dense()` function. The first parameter is the *input layer;* in this case we define an input layer of 100 points, which is used to define the input vector that will represent the initial noise for the generator.

The second parameter is the *units*, or artificial neurons, in the layers. In this case we define 256 units. The number of units will impact the number of features learned from the inputs. In this case, we will learn 256 different features from the inputs. The last parameter is the *activation function*, and because we are still working on a generator, we will use a `relu`. This is the same function defined in Python.

The next layer is *batch normalization*, and the goal of this layer is to stabilize the speed of the training. This is done by normalizing the activation which each mini-batch. The normalization of the inputs is done by re-centering and re-scaling the input data. Remember that AI works with numbers, and if the numbers become too big, this makes learning the data more complex. To avoid this problem, batch normalization fixes the mean variances of each layer input, which means that the number used as input is in a defined range, and this speeds up the process of learning. To achieve batch normalization, with the Flux framework you use the `BatchNorm()` function, which has just one parameter, the number of features being normalized (in this case 256). The generator continues to add two dense layers and one batch normalization layer; the normalization layer is in between the two dense layers. The dense layer has different values for the input size and the neuron layer because we tend to want the image the size of the MINST one. The last dense layer is responsible for image creation and in this layer, you have the input necessary to create the image of the MINST size.

In this case, the dense function is like this: `Dense(512, 784, tanh)`. 512 is the input size, which comes from the batch normalization layer. If you multiple the size of the MINST image 28*28 pixel, you get 784, so the dense layer will produce an image 28 by 28. The activation function is a *hyperbolic tangent*, or a *tanh*.

You have now defined the generator. The Flux framework is very different from the one used in Python, because the Flux framework was developed to be more compact. The spirit of Julia is to be a highly mathematical language and this spirit is transferred to the library as well.

Building the Discriminator

The other main component of the GAN is the discriminator, which is a simple neural network that classifies the images. The code for the discriminator is shown in Listing 5-10.

The code of the discriminator is very compact, and as you can see, it starts with a `Chain()` function. This functions adds a layer to the neural network that you want to design.

Listing 5-10. The Discriminator Code Written in Julia

```julia
function build_discriminator()
    print("Build the Discriminator")
    Chain(
        Dense(784, 512, leakyrelu),
        Dense(512, 256, leakyrelu),
        Dense(256, 1, σ)  # Output layer with single neuron for binary
        classification
    )
end
```

The stack of the layer in the case of the discriminator is essentially the opposite of what was done with the generator. The first `Dense()` or fully connected layer starts with an input layer of 784 points. If you recall the generator, this is the same size as the generated image. In the discriminator, the dense layers aim to reduce the image size with every stack. The discriminator is built with just three layers, and the first two have the same activation function, the `leakyrelu`. A Leaky Rectified Linear Unit, aka LeakyReLU, is an activation function that helps reduce the risk of overfitting a neural network.

This is done by allowing a small gradient in the negative section instead of being completely zero. The last layer uses a Sigmoid activation function, σ, which is sometimes called a logistic function. The function returns a value between 0 and 1, and essentially this is used to classify the image as real or fake. With the two neural networks created, you need to prepare the data and all the rest of the code that is necessary for the full neural network. You learn how to do that in the next section.

Building the Rest of the Neural Network

Up to now you just built two simple neural networks, but this alone is not enough to have a full GAN. Because you are building a simple vanilla GAN, you need to, first of all, download the MINST dataset. You can do this with the get_mnist_data() function. Listing 5-11 shows the code.

Listing 5-11. The Function to Collect the MNIST Data

```
function get_mnist_data()
    x_train, y_train = MLDatasets.MNIST.traindata()
    x_train = [Float32(reshape(Gray(img), 784)) for img in x_train]
    x_train = hcat(x_train...)
    x_train ./= 255.0
    return x_train, y_train
end
```

The get_mnist_data() function collects and downloads the MNIST dataset. It uses the MLDatasets package. The Julia community designed this dataset, which provides a common interface for accessing common machine learning datasets.

The *MLDatasets* package allows users to download and access the benchmark dataset. The dataset present in the package can be split into four categories:

- Graph datasets, which contain all the datasets with a graph structure.

- Text datasets, which contain all the datasets for the language models.

- Vision dataset, which contains all the vision-related datasets.

- Miscellaneous datasets, which are all the other datasets that didn't fall under the other classifications.

In this specific case, from the `MLDatasets` we use the MNIST one. You can load the dataset with this simple line: `x_train, y_train = MLDatasets.MNIST.traindata()`. This code associates the `x_train` and `y_train` variables with the training data from the MNIST dataset.

With the dataset loaded, you can start to preprocess the image. In this function, you can see some interesting Julia functionality. The first step is to convert all the train images into a single channel. To do that, you convert the images into gray ones, which creates images with only one channel. This makes it easier to learn the images themselves.

This line of code is responsible for reshaping and transforming the image from the MNIST dataset into a gray dataset:

```
x_train = [Float32(reshape(Gray(img), 784)) for img in x_train]
```

Let's analyze the code a little bit, because it offers some good learning points for the Julia syntax. First of all, the code creates a list of images. In Julia, you can use the syntax `[..]` with a specific operation inside to create a new list with the result of the previous operation.

The list is created using a `for` loop on all the images in the `x_train` dataset, `for img in x_train`. Every image is then reshaped and converted in a gray one and converted in a Float32. The images are reshaped to all the same size. In this case, we create the image with a size of 784, which indicates an image of 28x28 pixels in size. This is the same size as the final image created by the generator neural network and of course, is the same size as the input image for the discriminator. Because we reshape the image, we create a 1D array for a single image, which will be used in the next steps. The last part of the list comprehension is the Float32, which is used to convert the data of the image in a float, and this is important for the next steps.

In the next step, the `hcat(x_train...)` function horizontally concatenates all the flattened images. The result of the function is a matrix where each column represents a flattened image. With the new matrix created, you need to normalize it, which means that you create the pixel in a range between 0 and 1. To do that you essentially use this line of code `x_train ./= 255.0`, which divides every pixel value by 255.0. The result is a value between 0 and 1.

With the data load and preprocessed, you can define some hyperparameters, which are an essential step in the neural network. The parameters we are going to define in this example are as follows:

```
latent_dim = 100
batch_size = 128
epochs = 10000
lr = 0.0002
```

The first parameter (`latent_dim`) is the latent dimension, which is used to define the dimension of the noise array. In this case, this is similar to what we did in Python—we define a dimension of 100. The next hyperparameter is `batch_size`, which simply defines the number of images processed in each training iteration. The last two hyperparameters are the most important—epochs and `lr`. The epoch defines the number of training iterations, more epochs can learn more from the data but can lead to overfitting, where fewer epochs can't learn the underlying structure of the data. For this example, epochs is 10000. The learning rate, `lr`, defines the increment of the learning for the algorithm. This is a very important part of the generalization of the model. With the hyperparameters defined, it's now time to define the neural network optimizers. They are defined with these lines of codes:

```
opt_gen = ADAM(lr)
opt_disc = ADAM(lr)
```

The two lines of code define the ADAM (Adaptive Moment Estimation), which combines two gradient descent methodologies to give a more optimized gradient descent.

With the hyperparameter defined and indicated, you can now define the loss functions. The loss function is important because it's used to correct the training of the generator and the discriminator. This code uses a Binary Cross Entropy loss, which compares the predicted probability with the actual label. Listing 5-12 shows the loss function.

Listing 5-12. The Code to Define the Loss Function

```
function bce_loss(y_hat, y)
    return -mean(y*log(y_hat+1e-8) + (1- y)*log(1-y_hat+1e-8))
end
```

```
function discriminator_loss(real_output, fake_output)
    real_loss = bce_loss(real_output,ones(size(real_output)))
    fake_loss = bce_loss(fake_output,zeros(size(fake_output)))
    return real_loss+fake_loss
end

function generator_loss(fake_output)
    return bce_loss(fake_output, ones(size(fake_output)))
end
```

The bce_loss(y_hat,y) function compares the predicted probability, y_hat, with the actual label, y. The function implements the mathematical formula defining the Binary Cross Entropy. The bce_loss function is used to classify the image as real or fake. The bce_loss function is used in the discriminator_loss and generator_loss functions. The real_loss is used to calculate the loss for the real image. The parameters you send to the bce_loss are the real_output, which is all the real images. The second parameter is an array with ones, the size is the same as the real_output array. The bce_loss will return the value of the operation between 0 and 1 and calculate the distance between all the images and the value 1. A value near 1 indicates a high probability of the images being real. The calculation for fake_loss follows the same logic for real_loss. The difference is that you send it fake images. The last operation of the function is to sum the fake_loss and the real_loss, which is what the discriminator tries to minimize. The discriminator tries to have a value of 0, indicating that it is able to recognize when an image is fake.

The function that calculates the loss of the generator, generator_loss, is simpler than the one used to calculate the discriminator loss. The function calculates the loss using only the fake output because the generator's goal is to create an image that will be near to 1, which is an image that the discriminator will classify as real. With the basic functionality of the GANs ready, you need to prepare the code to train and run the GAN. Listing 5-13 shows the function and the code used for doing that.

Listing 5-13. The Code for Training the GAN

```
function train_step()
    noise = randn(Float32, latent_dim, batch_size)
    fake_images = generator(noise)
    idx = rand(1:size(real_images, 2), batch_size)
```

```
    real_batch = real_images[:, idx]
    real_output = discriminator(real_batch)
    fake_output = discriminator(fake_images)

    disc_loss = discriminator_loss(real_output, fake_output)
    gen_loss = generator_loss(fake_output)

    Flux.back!(disc_loss)
    Flux.update!(opt_disc, discriminator)

    Flux.back!(gen_loss)
    Flux.update!(opt_gen, generator)

    return disc_loss, gen_loss
end

for epoch in 1:epochs
    disc_loss, gen_loss = train_step()

    if epoch % 100 == 0
        println("Epoch $epoch | Discriminator Loss: $(disc_loss) | Generator
        Loss: $(gen_loss)")
    end

    if epoch % 1000 == 0
        noise = randn(Float32, latent_dim, 1)
        fake_image = reshape(generator(noise), 28, 28)
        fake_image = clamp.(fake_image, 0, 1)
        println("Generated sample image at epoch $epoch:")
        display(fake_image)
    end
end
```

Before you start to train the GAN, you need to initialize the generator and the
discriminator. To do that, you need to associate the function with some variables:

```
generator = build_generator()
discriminator = build_discriminator()
```

This code essentially initializes the network and creates two variables, one for the generator and one for the discriminator. You use it to train the network.

The function for training the GAN is `train_step()`. The first two lines of the function are used to call the generator. The first line creates the noise vector, `noise = randn(Float32, latent_dim, batch_size)`. It creates an array of a random values and uses the hyperparameter to define the latent dimension and the batch size. The result is a matrix of the size of the latent dimension for the batch size.

With the noise vector created, you can start to generate the first image. You need to remember that the GAN starts to generate the image using a random noise vector. In the code, the line used to generate the image is `fake_images=generator(noise)`, which uses the previously initialized network and generates the first fake images. You need to select a set of random real images to send to the discriminator for training. That is done with this line of the code: `idx=rand(1:size(real_images, 2),batch_size)`. This code generates a random index, and the range of the number is between 1 and size of the real images vector. With the number generated, you then select the batch of images from the real image vector, which is done using this line of code: `real_batch = real_images[:, idx]`. This will create a vector of the real images, from the start to the random index.

With that basic definition, you can start to train the discriminator. To do that you need to run the discriminator with the real and the fake images. Listing 5-14 shows the snippet of code that does this.

Listing 5-14. The Snippet of Code Used to Train the Discriminator

```
real_output = discriminator(real_batch)
fake_output = discriminator(fake_images)

disc_loss = discriminator_loss(real_output, fake_output)
gen_loss = generator_loss(fake_output)
```

The code is quite self-explanatory. It calls the discriminator to send the real and fake batches of data, and with the output, it computes the loss of the result, which is used to adjust the discriminator.

At this point, you have calculated the loss for both the neural network, and because you have built a GAN, you need to update the value for the neural network, the generator, and the discriminator. In Julia, you can use the *Flux* framework, one of the packages you installed. Flux is a library specifically designed for machine learning. It has all the tools you need. Listing 5-15 shows how to use Flux to create the backpropagation you need for your GAN.

Listing 5-15. The Flux Library Creates the Backpropagation and Updates the Loss Value for the Discriminator and the Generator

```
Flux.back!(disc_loss)
Flux.update!(opt_disc, discriminator)

Flux.back!(gen_loss)
Flux.update!(opt_gen, generator)
```

The code is the same for the generator and the discriminator; you use the back!() function from the Flux framework. This function uses the backpropagation to update the weight and biases; the values are updated using the loss calculated before. The back!() function sends the data back, but you need to use the update!() function, which will update the values for the generator and the discriminator, using the loss Adam optimizer defined earlier. In this way, you ensure that the discriminator and the generator will use the calculated loss and the optimizer. The function finishes returning the calculated loss for the generator and the discriminator.

With all the components in place, you can finally code the training part. This is done with the last part, as shown in Listing 5-16.

Listing 5-16. The Code for Training the GAN and Printing the Image

```
for epoch in 1:epochs
    disc_loss, gen_loss = train_step()

    if epoch % 100 == 0
        println("Epoch $epoch | Discriminator Loss: $(disc_loss) | Generator
        Loss: $(gen_loss)")
    end

    if epoch % 1000 == 0
        noise = randn(Float32, latent_dim, 1)
        fake_image = reshape(generator(noise), 28, 28)
        fake_image = clamp.(fake_image, 0, 1)
        println("Generated sample image at epoch $epoch:")
        display(fake_image)
    end
end
```

The code is a simple for loop, which iterates starting at 1 to all the epochs you defined in the hyperparameters. The loop essentially calls the `train_step()` function, which is the one used to train the discriminator and the generator. At every 100 epochs, the code will print out the image, similar to what Python does.

Final Thoughts

You have seen how to build a GAN using Python and Julia, and I chose to explain how to build a vanilla GAN so that you get a basic understanding of how a GAN is built and works.

Since the introduction of GAN, many researchers have studied how to apply it to different areas. GAN is mainly used for image manipulation. Some of its uses include:

- **Image generation:** You saw this with the vanilla GAN, which creates a new image starting from some basic image and has the GAN generate a new one.

- **Image translation:** In this case, the GAN transforms basic images by adding external features, such as adding glasses or changing the expression of a face.

- **Semantic image translation:** This type of GAN generates an image using a sketch. This technique is used in self-driving cars. The GAN generates a map used by the car.

- **Super resolution:** In this case, the GAN improves the quality of the input image or video. This is used to enhance the video quality of the image resolution to restore old images.

- **Video prediction:** The GAN predicts the next frame of a video, which can be used to reconstruct a damaged video.

- **Style transfer:** The GAN can transfer a style from one image to another, which can be used to produce an image with a different style. This is used to generate computer art.

- **Synthetic data generation:** The GAN can be used to generate synthetic data. Because the generated data is similar but not the same, this data can be used to train other machine learning or artificial intelligence models without violating privacy or trademark laws.

- **Anomaly detection:** The GAN can be used to identify anomalies in an image. One of the most famous uses is f-AnoGAN, which is trained with a valid image and then highlights any anomalies on the new image. This particular GAN is used in the medical field to indicate tumors and other potential medical issues.

These are just some of the uses of GANs. The capacity to generate new data starting with a simple noise and to shape the data using a "discriminator" make this architecture very flexible and allows it to be used in different areas. GANs are also used in unethical ways, such to create deepfakes to fool humans.

Conclusion

This chapter implemented the first generative architecture of the book. It started with GANs, which are at the heart of most of modern architectures and other multimodal AI approaches. GANs can generate video and images. Sites like "thispersondoesnotexist" show how GANs generate synthetic yet realistic images. In the chapter, you learned how Julia and Python can be used to realize this architecture and you learned about the differences in terms of code. Julia as a language was born specifically to solve this type of problem and the framework is more compact. This chapter is just the first step in your journey. Now that you know the basic architecture and how to train a GAN, you can go out into the wild and learn how other GAN architectures work and are implemented.

CHAPTER 6

Autoencoders

The previous chapter introduced Generative Adversarial Networks (GANs), which is specific deep learning architecture learns the *latent representation,* or the *coding,* of the data. Another architecture that learns the latent representation of the data are *autoencoders.* Both architectures learn the latent representation of the data, but the ways that they understand and represent the data are different, and because of that the generated data is different. One of the main differences is the fact that autoencoders *copy* the input data, whereas GANs generate random data that is *similar,* but not the same. In this chapter, you will learn about autoencoders and how they can be used to generate new data.

Introduction to Autoencoders

Autoencoders use unsupervised machine learning to determine the *latent variable* of the data. This variable represents the important information of the data. The information learned is used by the autoencoder to *copy* the input data into the output data. Recall from Chapter 5 that GANs don't copy the data, they learn how to reproduce similar data. An autoencoder is built using two parts—an *encoder,* $h = f(x)$ and a *decoder,* that essentially tries to reproduce the input $r = g(h)$. An autoencoder is successful if it learns to set the value for $g(f(x)) = x\ \ x$.

The autoencoder uses an encoder-decoder architecture, but there is one main difference between an autoencoder and an encoder-decoder architecture. With an encoder-decoder architecture, the encoder will learn which features are the most important and use that information as input for the decoder. The encoder-decoder is normally used in different types of architecture like RNN and CNN, but they will not use the data to generate new data. In most cases, the data in the output produced by an encoder-decoder architecture is different from the data in the input. An example of the usage of an encoder-decoder application can be found in a model like the U-Net one, where the encoder extracts features and uses them to learn the semantics of the different pixels. With this knowledge, the decoder will classify the different areas of the images. This is useful when you want to provide an object recognition of the elements of the image. The objects are recognized using a supervised learning technique.

An autoencoder, on the other hand, uses an unsupervised learning technique. The goal of an autoencoder is to reconstruct the input data, which means that the autoencoder will generate data using the input data. To summarize, the encoder-decoder uses a supervised learning algorithm to learn, and an autoencoder uses an unsupervised learning methodology to learn the data and then reconstruct the input. The autoencoder architecture is represented in Figure 6-1.

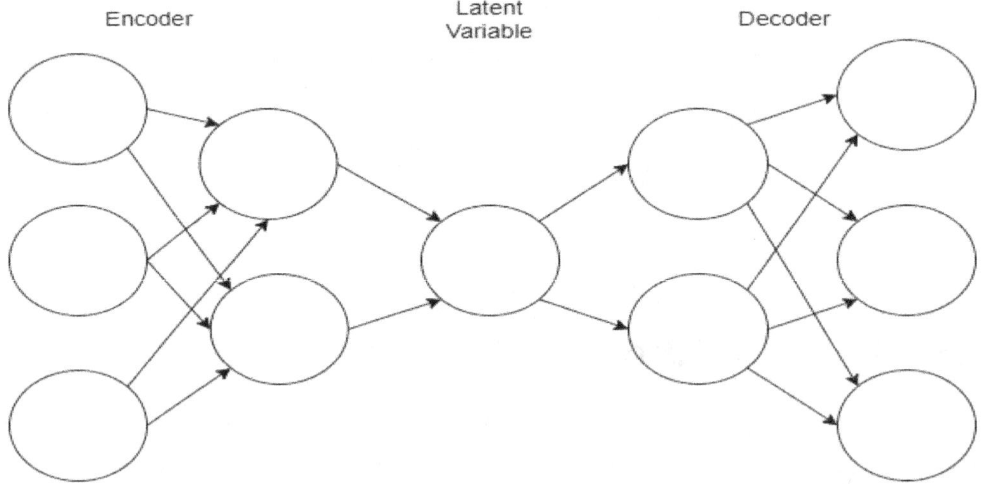

Figure 6-1. *The representation of an autoencoder*

The encoder reduces the input data using a dimensionality reduction, in order to learn and isolate the latent space of the input data. Then the decoder, starting from the latent space, reproduces and generates a copy of the input data. Autoencoders were introduced by Rumelhart et al., in the paper titled "*Learning Internal Representations by Error Propagation.*" The autoencoder uses an unsupervised manner to learn the efficient representation of the data.

Autoencoders can be seen as a special type of feedforward network because the input data goes through the entire network, but there is no loop in the node. Because of that, you can train the autoencoders using the classic technique used for the feedforward network, for example, a mini-batch descendent gradient.

One of the differences when training an autoencoder versus the classical feedforward network is that with the autoencoder, you can use *recirculation* to train the autoencoder. This algorithm compares the activation of the autoencoder with its input of the activations on the reconstructed input. Recirculation is rarely used in machine learning training, but it seems biologically better than back-propagation.

In their simplest form, the two parts of the autoencoder architecture are two simple neural networks. When they perform simple linear operations, you get what is called a *linear autoencoder*. In this case, the autoencoder will drop out all the nonlinear operations, which makes the autoencoder as a generalization of a Principal Component Analysis (PCA). This is because the autoencoder will reduce the data to only the most important features.

You can also have what is called a *stacked autoencoder*, or a *deep-autoencoder*. In this case, the layers are stacked one over each other, which allows them to learn better and better represent the data.

Different Types of Autoencoders

The aim of an autoencoder is to copy the input data in the output. But when you use an autoencoder, you are not typically interested in the output of the decoder, instead, the goal of the autoencoder is to perform an input task, hoping that will result in the decoder copying only the useful properties.

One of the ways to collect only the important features from the autoencoder is to reduce the dimension. These types of autoencoders are called *undercomplete* encoders.

The idea behind this type of autoencoder is simple. The autoencoder is forced to learn fewer features than the input, which forces it to learn the most salient features of the training data. To achieve that, the learning process will minimize the loss function, and a function can be written like this:

$$L\left(x, g\left(f\left(x\right)\right)\right)$$

Essentially you want to learn the loss function, L, which penalizes fo . The loss function can be calculated using, for example, a mean squared error. If you have a linear decoder and as a loss function a mean squared error, the autoencoders will act similarly to a PCA.

The undercomplete autoencoders can be used to learn the most important features of the data distribution, which makes the autoencoders similar to a PCA. Essentially the autoencoder is used for dimensionality reduction.

The problem with an undercomplete autoencoder is essentially the fact that the autoencoder can't learn anything useful when the encoder and the decoder are given too much capacity.

The same problem can happen when you have an *overcomplete* autoencoder, which is a type of autoencoder that has hidden code, aka latent space, or dimensions greater than the input. In this case, the autoencoder will not learn anything useful.

To train a successful autoencoder you need to choose the dimension of the latent space for the encoder and the decoder, based on the complexity of the distribution you want to learn and model. This task can be very complex, but the *regularized autoencoders* help solve this problem.

The regularized autoencoders don't limit the model capacity because they use a loss function that encourages the models to not limit their capacity and to only copy the input on the output. This translates into the autoencoder using other properties to learn how to model the input data. These properties can include the sparsity of the representation. Because of the importance of these types of autoencoders, the next section describes them in a bit more detail. The first one you learn about is the sparse autoencoder.

Sparse Autoencoders

To be effective as an autoencoder, you need to be able to not only learn how to copy the input on the output, but also how to model the data.

If the autoencoder just learns to copy input to output, it can lose the capacity to generalize the model, and this means that if you change something in the model, the autoencoder is no longer able to reproduce it.

This creates a variance/tradeoff bias, because the autoencoder needs to balance the capacity to exactly copy the input data on the output, but at the same time must be generic enough to be used with similar data. To solve this balance, you can add sparsity to the hidden activation. This creates a different type of autoencoder called a sparse autoencoder. The sparse autoencoder adds sparsity to create a bottleneck of the information. To achieve that, the loss function is constructed in a way that penalizes the activation functions. The sparsity can be forced with an L1 regularization or a Kullback-Leibler (KL) divergence between the neurons and the probability distribution of the data.

The L1 regularization technique is applied to the weight of a neural network. The technique minimizes a loss function compromising both the primary loss function and a penalty on the L1 norm of the weights.

Using the autoencoder formula defined in the previous paragraph, a sparse autoencoder can be represented in this way:

$$L\big(x, g(f(x))\big) + \Omega(h)$$

In this case, you add the "penalty" $\Omega(h)$ to the loss function. The usage of the penalty, $\Omega(h)$, can be seen as a regularizer term added to a feedforward network, where the primary task is to copy the input to the output and perform a supervised task that depends on these sparse features.

Sparse autoencoders are used to learn features for another task, generally a classification.

Sparse Autoencoder with Python

Up to now, you have learned about the theory behind sparse autoencoders, but the goal of the book is to teach you to write code to build generative artificial intelligence. Listing 6-1 shows the code for a sparse autoencoder in Python.

Listing 6-1. An Example of a Sparse Autoencoder

```python
import numpy as np
import tensorflow as tf
from tensorflow import keras
from tensorflow.keras import layers
import matplotlib.pyplot as plt

(x_train, _), (x_test, _) = keras.datasets.mnist.load_data() x_train = x_
train.reshape((x_train.shape[0], -1)).astype('float32') / 255.0 x_test =
x_test.reshape((x_test.shape[0], -1)).astype('float32') / 255.0

input_dim = 784
hidden_dim = 64
sparsity_level = 0.05
lambda_sparse = 0.1
```

```python
inputs = layers.Input(shape=(input_dim,))
encoded = layers.Dense(hidden_dim, activation='sigmoid')(inputs)
decoded = layers.Dense(input_dim, activation='sigmoid')(encoded)

autoencoder = keras.Model(inputs, decoded)
encoder = keras.Model(inputs, encoded)

def sparse_loss(y_true, y_pred):
    mse_loss = tf.reduce_mean(keras.losses.MeanSquaredError()      (y_true,
    y_pred))
    hidden_layer_output = encoder(y_true)
    mean_activation = tf.reduce_mean(hidden_layer_output, axis=0)
    kl_divergence = tf.reduce_sum(sparsity_level *          tf.math.
    log(sparsity_level / (mean_activation + 1e-10)) +
                        (1 - sparsity_level) * tf.math.log((1
                        -sparsity_level) / (1 - mean_activation +
                        1e-10)))
    return mse_loss + lambda_sparse * kl_divergence

autoencoder.compile(optimizer='adam', loss=sparse_loss)

history = autoencoder.fit(x_train, x_train, epochs=50, batch_size=256,
shuffle=True)

reconstructed = autoencoder.predict(x_test)

n = 10 plt.figure(figsize=(20, 4)) for i in range(n):
    ax = plt.subplot(2, n, i + 1)
    plt.imshow(x_test[i].reshape(28, 28), cmap='gray')
    plt.title("Original Image") plt.axis('off')

    ax = plt.subplot(2, n, i + 1 + n)
    plt.imshow(reconstructed[i].reshape(28, 28), cmap='gray')
    plt.title("Reconstructed Image")
    plt.axis('off')

plt.show()
```

When you run the code, you see the result shown in Figure 6-2. The autoencoder reconstructs the image.

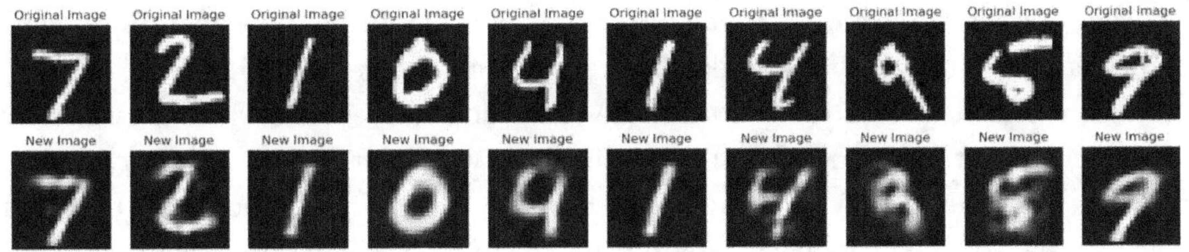

Figure 6-2. *The result of the sparse autoencoder*

To understand how this works, let's analyze the code. After importing the necessary library, you need to create the train and test datasets.

```
(x_train, _), (x_test, _) = keras.datasets.mnist.load_data() x_train =
x_train.reshape((x_train.shape[0], -1)).astype('float32') / 255.0
x_test = x_test.reshape((x_test.shape[0], -1)).astype('float32') / 255.0
```

The first line downloads the MNIST dataset. Keras has a utility to do that, and the line `keras.datasets.mnist.load_data()` downloads and associates the MNIST and splits between the train and test dataset.

Because the dataset is essentially a set of images, you need to reshape and normalize the data. The `x_train.reshape((x_train.shape[0], -1)).astype('float32') / 255.0`, code shows the operation for reshaping and normalization of the data. The command is used to translate the image in a flat array of the size of 28x28=784. This creates a flat array of numbers between 0 and 255. This operation essentially reshapes the data in order to normalize it. You divide the number by 255, which will provide a float number between 0 and 1. This creates a dataset you can use to learn and encode/decode the data. (Remember that every AI or ML model uses numbers to represent reality, for this reason it is important to create and prepare the data.) After defining the dataset, you define the parameters of the models, which are the hyperparameters. Changing the values can drastically change the output of the model. The first test defines these parameters:

```
input_dim = 784
hidden_dim = 64
sparsity_level = 0.05
lambda_sparse = 0.1
```

The parameter indicates the input dimension, which indicates how many inputs are in the network. This is easy to calculate because the image has a size of 28 by 28, and the input dimension is 784. `hidden_dim` indicates the hidden dimension, which is essentially the dimension for the latent space. For this first test, we move this to 64. The last two parameters are the sparsity level and the sparsity regulation weight. The `sparsity_level` defines the average activation layer for the hidden neurons, which are the neurons for the latent space. The other variable is `lamba_sparse`, which defines the weight factor for the sparsity penalty term in the loss function, controlling how strongly sparsity is enforced. This value defines the sparsity and how the autoencoder will learn the features from the input.

After the definition of the hyperparameter, it is now time to define the basic encoder/decoder architecture. This architecture is defined along these lines:

```
inputs = layers.Input(shape=(input_dim,))
encoded = layers.Dense(hidden_dim, activation='sigmoid')(inputs)
decoded = layers.Dense(input_dim, activation='sigmoid') (encoded)

autoencoder = keras.Model(inputs, decoded)
encoder = keras.Model(inputs, encoded)
```

The first line of code `inputs = layers.Input(shape=(input_dim,))` is used to create the input layers. In this case, we create an input layer of 784 features, which is essentially the dimension of the flattened image, 28 by 28.

The other two lines are responsible for creating the encoder and decoder neural network, and they are essentially similar. The difference is in the neuron we will connect to the Dense layer. In the case of an encoder, because we start with the input and we scale the dimension, we have a dense layer with the size of the hidden dimension(in this case 64). In the case of the decoder, the dense layer has an output of 784, because this is the dimension of the image you want to regenerate. Both neural networks use a Sigmoid activation function. The last difference between the two neural networks is what they get in input. In the case of an encoder, the input is essentially the input layer, while in the decoder the input is the encoder itself. This will connect the two networks and create the encoder/decoder architecture.

The sparse autoencoder is a type that learns the sparsity to force the Kullback-Leibler (KL) divergence. To do that, you need to have a function that can be used to force this divergence. In this code, that function is `sparse_loss`. The code for the function is as follows:

```
def sparse_loss(y_true, y_pred):
    mse_loss = tf.reduce_mean(keras.losses.MeanSquaredError()    (y_true,
    y_pred))
    hidden_layer_output = encoder(y_true)
    mean_activation = tf.reduce_mean(hidden_layer_output, axis=0)
    kl_divergence = tf.reduce_sum(sparsity_level *          tf.math.
log(sparsity_level / (mean_activation + 1e-10)) +
                        (1 - sparsity_level) * tf.math.log((1
                        -sparsity_level) / (1 - mean_activation +
                        1e-10)))
    return mse_loss + lambda_sparse * kl_divergence
```

The function calculates the Mean Squared Error (MSE) between the original data, y_
true, and the predicted data, y_pred. After that, the code will calculate the hidden layer
activation and the mean for the activation. Finally, with all the information about the
error and the activation calculated for the hidden layer, it calculates the KL divergence.
The KL divergence measures the difference between the mean activation and the desired
sparsity.

The function will end with the return of the new loss, which is the sum of the mean
squared error, and the lambda sparse, all multiplied by the KL divergence. At this point,
you have all the pieces in place and the next step is to compile the autoencoder before
the training phase. This is done with this line of code `autoencoder.compile(optimize`
`r='adam',loss=sparse_loss)`. The autoencoder will use an Adam optimizer and the
loss will be the `sparse_loss` function defined before. This will ensure that we train the
autoencoder using a sparsity on the data. At this point the rest of the code is used to train
the autoencoder and reconstruct the input data. The result can be seen in Figure 6-1.

If you play with the hyperparameters, you can see how the autoencoder responds.
For example you can update the value of the hidden dimension, which means the latent
space will learn more variable. You can also change the sparsity level and the lambda
spare value. The new values are as follows:

```
input_dim = 784
hidden_dim = 128
sparsity_level = 0.5
lambda_sparse = 0.01
```

If you run the autoencoder again, you will see that the images are clearer and closer to the originals, as shown in Figure 6-3.

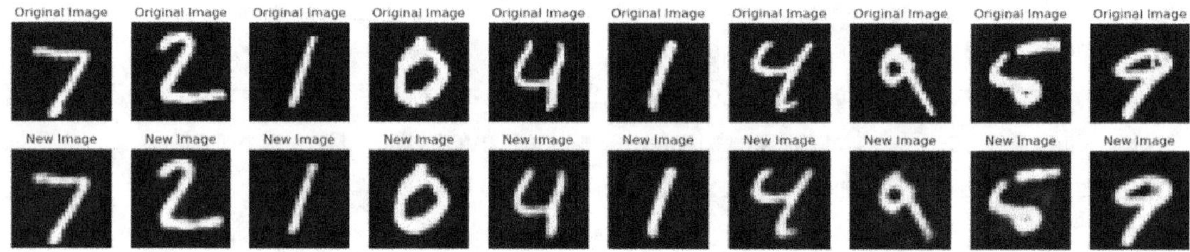

Figure 6-3. *The images reconstructed with the new hyperparameter*

The next section explains how to write the same architecture using Julia.

Sparse Autoencoder in Julia

The code for the sparse autoencoder in Julia is shown in Listing 6-2.

Listing 6-2. The Sparse Autoencoder in Julia

```julia
using Flux: DataLoader, trainable
using Flux.Optimisers: ADAM, update!, setup
using Flux
using Statistics
using MLDatasets: MNIST
using Images, ImageShow
using Zygote using Plots

function load_mnist(batch_size::Int = 128)
    imgs = MNIST(split=:train).features
    labels = Float32.(MNIST(split=:train).targets)
    imgs = reshape(imgs, 28 * 28, :) .|> Float32
    imgs ./= 255.0f0
    train_loader = DataLoader((imgs, labels),     batchsize=batch_size,
    shuffle=true)

    test_imgs = MNIST(split=:test).features
    test_labels = Float32.(MNIST(split=:test).targets)
    test_imgs = reshape(test_imgs, 28 * 28, :) .|> Float32
```

```julia
    test_imgs ./= 255.0f0
    test_loader = DataLoader((test_imgs, test_labels),
    batchsize=batch_size)

    return train_loader, test_loader
end

function sparse_autoencoder(input_size::Int,hidden_size::Int)
    println("Building Sparse Autoencoder")
    encoder = Chain( Dense(input_size, 512, relu), Dense(512, hidden_
    size, relu) )

    decoder = Chain(
        Dense(hidden_size, 512, relu),
        Dense(512, input_size, relu)
    )
    model = Chain(encoder, decoder)
    return model, encoder
end

function loss_sparsity(x, model, encoder, sparsity_weight, sparsity_target)
    encoded = encoder(x) decoded = model(x) reconstruction_loss = Flux.
    Losses.binarycrossentropy(decoded, x)

    avg_activation = mean(encoded, dims=2)
    avg_activation = vec(avg_activation)
    avg_activation = clamp.(avg_activation, 1e-6, 1 - 1e-6)

    sparsity_penalty = sparsity_weight * sum(sparsity_target      *log.
    (sparsity_target ./ avg_activation) +(1 .- sparsity_target) .* log.((1
    .- sparsity_target) ./ (1 .- avg_activation)))

    return reconstruction_loss + sparsity_penalty
end

function train!(model, encoder, data_loader, opt_state, sparsity_weight,
sparsity_target, epochs::Int)

println("Starting training...")
```

```julia
for epoch in 1:epochs
    losses = []
    for (x, _) in data_loader
        loss_value, grads = Zygote.withgradient(model) do m
            loss_sparsity(x, m, encoder, sparsity_weight, sparsity_target)
        end

        push!(losses, loss_value)

        update!(opt_state, model, grads[1])
    end

    avg_loss = mean(losses)
    if epoch % 10 == 0
        println("Epoch $epoch, Average Loss: $avg_loss")
    end
end
end

function visualize_sample(original, decoded)
    orig_img = reshape(original, 28, 28)
    decoded_img = reshape(decoded, 28, 28)

    p1 = heatmap(orig_img, title="Original Image", color=:viridis,
    axis=false)
    p2 = heatmap(decoded_img, title="Reconstructed Image", color=:viridis,
    axis=false)

    fig = plot(p1, p2, layout=(1,2), size=(600,300))
display(fig)
end
function main()
    input_size = 28 * 28
    hidden_size = 100
    batch_size = 256
    epochs = 150
    sparsity_target = 0.1f0
    sparsity_weight = 0.001f0
```

```
    train_loader, test_loader = load_mnist(batch_size)
    model, encoder = sparse_autoencoder(input_size, hidden_size)

    opt_state = setup(ADAM(1e-4), model)

    train!(model, encoder, train_loader, opt_state,
    sparsity_weight, sparsity_target, epochs)

    println("Visualizing test sample...")
    test_data, _ = first(test_loader)
    sample = test_data[:, 1]
    decoded_sample = model(sample)
    visualize_sample(sample, decoded_sample)

    return model, encoder
end

model, encoder = main()
```

Like the Python code, this code is organized by function and we will calculate the sparsity in a specific function. The code will produce an image like the one in Figure 6-4. The image in this case is rendered differently but shows how the autoencoder can reconstruct an image starting with the original.

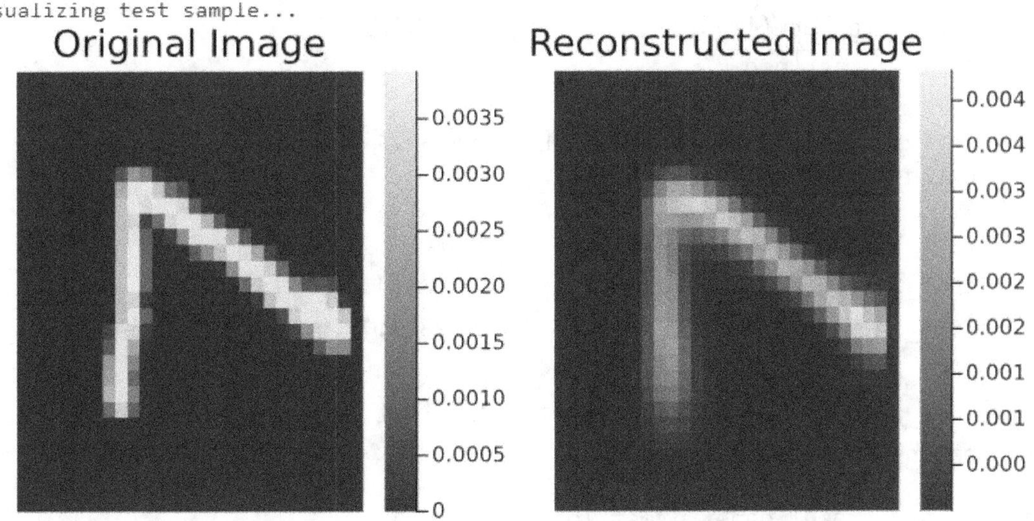

Figure 6-4. *The reconstructed image from the sparse autoencoder in Julia*

Let's analyze the code to see how to use Julia to write a sparse autoencoder. The `main()` function calls the other function and defines the hyperparameter. In this case, we define these hyperparameters:

```
input_size = 28 * 28
hidden_size = 100
batch_size = 256
epochs = 150
sparsity_target = 0.1f0
sparsity_weight = 0.001f0
```

Because we use a MNIST dataset, the image will be 28*28 and the `input_size` parameter indicates the dimension of the image. The other parameters have the same purpose as in the Python example. The `main()` function is responsible for calling some other function. The `load_mnist()` function is used to load the MNIST dataset. This function is shown in Listing 6-3 .

Listing 6-3. The load_mnist Function of Julia

```
function load_mnist(batch_size::Int = 128)
1     imgs = MNIST(split=:train).features
2     labels = Float32.(MNIST(split=:train).targets)

3     imgs = reshape(imgs, 28 * 28, :) .|> Float32
4     imgs ./= 255.0f0

5     train_loader = DataLoader((imgs, labels),
      batchsize=batch_size, shuffle=true)

6     test_imgs = MNIST(split=:test).features
7     test_labels = Float32.(MNIST(split=:test).targets)
8     test_imgs = reshape(test_imgs, 28 * 28, :) .|> Float32
9     test_imgs ./= 255.0f0
10    test_loader = DataLoader((test_imgs, test_labels),
      batchsize=batch_size)

11    return train_loader, test_loader
end
```

Line 1 loads the image from the MNIST dataset, which will collect the image on the size of 28*28. Line 2 collects the labels of the target. We convert this as a number from 0 to 9, because the MNIST dataset will give us only the number between 0 and 9. Line 3 is used to reshape the images. We essentially create 28*28 images. Here is one of the interesting functions of Julia:

```
|> Float32
```

This syntax converts the value of Float32. In a simple world, Julia will convert the number that forms the image on a datatype Float32.

Line 4 is used to *normalize* the image. This is the same process we follow in Python. For efficiency with learning and representation, you need to have small numbers because they use fewer bytes. For this reason we convert the number on a range between 0 and 1, in this way we can have small number with the representation we need and the algorithm is better at learning.

Line 5 is used to create the `DataLoader`. This is a Flux utility and is used to create the data in batches. The data loader will create the batch of images used for training the model. The size is defined in the `batch_size` hyperparameter. In our case, there are 256 images per batch. The parameter `shuffle=true` is used to shuffle the images so that the imaged are randomly chosen and used for training. This line concludes the creation of the dataset for the training.

From lines 6 to 10 we do exactly the same steps but for the test image dataset. The difference in this case is on the `DataLoader` created on Line 10. In this case we don't want to shuffle the image, because we want to have a controlled dataset for our test, and this is why we don't use the shuffle parameters. With the dataset created, you can now create the sparse autoencoder. This is done with the function shown in Listing 6-4. This code uses Flux to create the two components—the encoder and the decoder.

Listing 6-4. The Code to Create the Sparse Autoencoder in Julia

```
function sparse_autoencoder(input_size::Int,hidden_size::Int)
1    println("Building Sparse Autoencoder")
2    encoder = Chain(
3        Dense(input_size, 512, relu),
4        Dense(512,hidden_size, relu)
5        )
6    decoder = Chain(
```

```
7          Dense(hidden_size, 512, relu),
8          Dense(512, input_size, relu)
9          )

10    model = Chain(encoder, decoder)
11    return model, encoder
end
```

This code is quite simple. As you can see, it uses the Chain library to create both components of the autoencoder. Both are Dense, which means that all the layers are fully connected, and this is done because autoencoders are a special type of feedforward network.

The encoder, defined in lines 2 to 5, gets the input data and compresses the latent space. This is used to extract the important features from the data—what you want to copy with the autoencoder. In the encoder, the input_size and hidden_size hyperparameters are used. As you know, the encoder part on an autoencoder is used to reduce the input to a smaller dimension, because you want to force the encoder to learn only the important features that will be used to reproduce the data. Because the data can't be linear, you use a ReLU activation function. This helps capture nonlinear data as well.

The decoder is used to rebuild the data, starting from the compressed data and reverting back to the original size. The model always uses the Chain library, and as shown in line 10, this will create the full autoencoder using the encoder and the decoder to build up the model.

You have built the autoencoder and prepared the dataset. You now need to add sparsity to the loss function, which is done using the loss_sparsity function, shown in Listing 6-5.

Listing 6-5. The Loss Function with Sparsity

```
function loss_sparsity(x, model, encoder, sparsity_weight, sparsity_target)
1     encoded = encoder(x)
2     decoded = model(x)
3     reconstruction_loss =          Flux.Losses.binarycrossentropy(decoded, x)
4     avg_activation = mean(encoded, dims=2)
5     avg_activation = vec(avg_activation)
6     avg_activation = clamp.(avg_activation, 1e-6, 1 - 1e-6)
```

```
6    sparsity_penalty = sparsity_weight * sum(sparsity_target * log.
     (sparsity_target ./ avg_activation) + (1 .- sparsity_target) .* log.
     ((1 .- sparsity_target) ./ (1 .- avg_activation)))

8    return reconstruction_loss + sparsity_penalty
end
```

The `loss_sparsity` function is used to calculate the total loss, which is used for the training, and at the same time to calculate the sparsity penalty.

The function gets the input x, which is essentially the data you want to reconstruct, and is obtained directly from the training `DataLoader`. The input is passed to the encoder and the decoder, which is done in lines 1 and 2. Line 1 is the encoder, where the input is encoded and the important features are extracted from the model. Line 2 is where you reconstruct the data from the input.

At this point, we calculate the reconstruction loss. We use the Binary Cross Entropy Loss (BCE) to calculate this, which is done on line 3. As you can see, we use a Flux library, and the loss is calculated between the decoded data and the original input of the data, x.

Using Binary Cross Entropy Loss (BCE) is normal when you have normalized data, between 0 and 1. This applies a heavy penalization to the wrong prediction, which is normal and used with autoencoders.

The BCE function will provide a lower loss when the data is more similar, which means the higher is the loss, the more different the data. With the loss calculated, you need to calculate the *activation average* for the neuron. This is very important when you want to apply sparsity to the data. The average activation is just the mean value of the output across the entire batch. The average activation is very important because it encourages the sparsity. You need to reduce the dimension of the data to only the important feature, and you want most of the neurons to be inactive. That means you want that most of the neurons to be close to 0. The activation average is calculated on line 4. The result in Julia is a 2D matrix, because we use the `dims=2` parameter on the function, but because the mathematical operation used in the Kullback-Leibler (KL) Divergence uses a 1D vector, we use the code in line 5 to flatten the array from an 2D matrix to a 1D vector.

Line 6 closes the work by calculating the activation average. In this case, we use clamping, which prevents division by zero. The next operation calculates the sparsity penalty for the data, which is done on line 6. The sparsity penalty calculates the Kullback-Leibler divergence, which measures the difference between the average activation and the sparsity target defined in the hyperparameter. This calculation is used to make the model choose the value closer to the sparsity target. This will make the model more selective as to which data it learns. With all the data calculated, you can now return the loss value. This is done by adding the reconstruction loss to the sparsity loss.

You now need to define the function that will be used to train the autoencoder. This is done using the `train!` function, which is shown in Listing 6-6.

Listing 6-6. The Function Used to Train the Sparse Autoencoder

```
function train!(model, encoder, data_loader, opt_state, sparsity_weight,
sparsity_target, epochs::Int)
1     println("Starting training...")

2     for epoch in 1:epochs
3         losses = []
4         for (x, _) in data_loader
5             loss_value, grads = Zygote.withgradient(model)do m
6                 loss_sparsity(x, m, encoder, sparsity_
                  weight,sparsity_target)
7             end
8             push!(losses, loss_value)
9             update!(opt_state, model, grads[1])
10        end
11        avg_loss = mean(losses)
12        if epoch % 10 == 0
13            println("Epoch $epoch, Average Loss:$avg_loss")
14        end
15    end
end
```

The `train!` function will operate like any other train function. It will use the input parameter to go over the data and execute the training. This function has some key considerations you need to understand. Line 4 will interact over batches collected from the DataLoader. In this case, they are 256 images. Line 5 will calculate the gradient and the loss. We do that using the Zygote package from Julia, and in this moment we will calculate the loss and the sparsity on the data, where the gradient will be calculated and stored in the grads variable. Line 8 stores the loss value, which will be used to calculate the average in the future. Line 9 will update the model parameter using the gradient. We use grads[1] to ensure that only the model gradients are passed. Lines 11 to 14 calculate the loss for every epoch but will print out the loss only every 10 epochs.

You have now learned about all the important functions you need for a sparse autoencoder, so it's time to consider the main function you will use to build the autoencoder. This code is shown in Listing 6-7.

Listing 6-7. The Main Function for the Sparse Autoencoder

```
function main()
1     input_size = 28 * 28
2     hidden_size = 100
3     batch_size = 256
4     epochs = 150
5     sparsity_target = 0.1f0
6     sparsity_weight = 0.001f0
7     train_loader, test_loader = load_mnist(batch_size)
8     model, encoder = sparse_autoencoder(input_size, hidden_size)
9     opt_state = setup(ADAM(1e-4), model)
10    train!(model, encoder, train_loader, opt_state, sparsity_weight,
      sparsity_target, epochs)
11    println("Visualizing test sample...")
12    test_data, _ = first(test_loader)
13    sample = test_data[:, 1]
14    decoded_sample = model(sample)
15    visualize_sample(sample, decoded_sample)
16    return model, encoder
end
```

The code for the main function is essentially a call for the other function built until now. Line 9 defines the optimizer for the model. This examples uses ADAM (Adaptive Moment Estimation), because this algorithm will adjust the learning rate, and this will allow the functionality to learn the data better. In our case we use a learning rate of 0.0001, which will define how much we update the weight of the input during the training. My suggestion is to experiment with this value and see how the result changes. The `setup` function is a Flux function and the goal is to set up and use the optimizer we defined in the model. The optimizer will be used during the training in particular when the code calls the `update!` function in the `train!` function.

Your sparse autoencoder is ready and built, and you saw the result in Figure 6-3. Let's now move to another type the autoencoder, the denoising autoencoder.

Denoising Autoencoder

Denoising autoencoders learn important features without the artificial noise you add to the original data. Like other autoencoders, they use an unsupervised learning algorithm to learn the important features of the data.

The idea behind the denoising autoencoder is similar to the idea behind the sparse autoencoder, because you don't want the autoencoder to learn all the small details of the data. With a denoising autoencoder, you add "noise," which is used to make the autoencoder learn only the important features of the data and remove the details that can lead to overfitting. Conceptually, you can see a denoising autoencoder in Figure 6-5, and you can see the added "noise" on the original data before the data is processed. This pushes the decoder to remove the corrupted data and forces the autoencoder to only learn the original data.

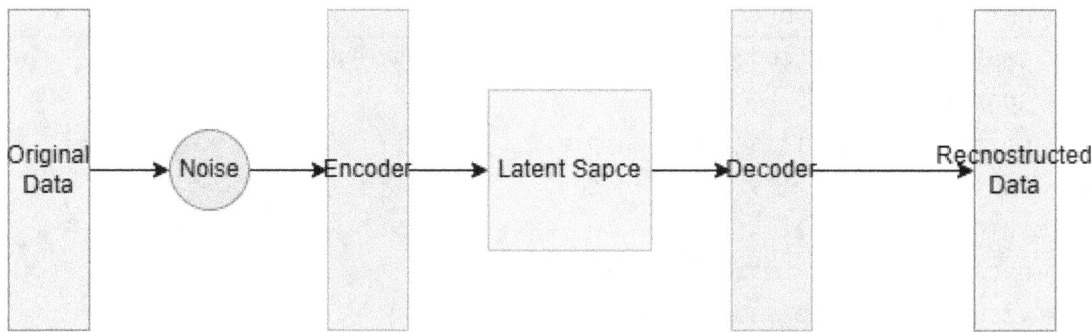

Figure 6-5. *The logical schema for a denoising autoencoder*

As you can see, the denoising autoencoder adds noise before it sends the data to the encoder. This is similar to what you do in the sparse autoencoder, because when you learn the loss, you concentrate on the important features and remove the noise from the original data.

The denoising autoencoder—rather than add a sparsity of the data, Ω—changes the reconstruction error in terms of the loss function. Mathematically speaking, a normal autoencoder tries to minimize the loss function:

$$L\big(x, g(f(x))\big)$$

In the formula, the loss function L penalizes the function $g(f(x))$ if the result is too dissimilar to x. This pushes the function to produce an identical value of the input.

The denoising autoencoder, *DAE*, tries to minimize the data with the noise. Mathematically you can change the previous formula to this one:

$$L\big(x, g(f(\tilde{x}))\big)$$

In this case, the function tries to penalize the loss of the function for the $\tilde{x}$ this noisy corrupted data. The denoising autoencoder needs to learn how to remove the noise, and this pushes the autoencoder to only learning the important data.

Denoising autoencoders are very useful because of this capacity to remove the noise. They can reconstruct corrupted data. Some practical applications are image denoising, which is useful when you need to reconstruct images with low resolution or that are captured with a lot of noise. The denoising autoencoder can learn what the data should be and then reproduce it. The next section explains how to build a denoising autoencoder.

Denoising Autoencoder in Python

This section writes the code for a denoising autoencoder, which will be different than what you did done for the sparse autoencoder. The main change is how the autoencoder is built. The denoise autoencoder is represented in Listing 6-8.

Listing 6-8. The New Denoising Autoencoder in Python

```
class Denoise_Autoencoder(Model):
    def init(self):
        super().__init__()

        activation_func = tf.keras.activations.leaky_relu

        self.encoder =    tf.keras.Sequential([
        layers.Conv2D(64, (3, 3),
```

```python
            activation=activation_func,
            padding='same', strides=2,
            input_shape=(28, 28, 1)),
    layers.BatchNormalization(),
    layers.Conv2D(32, (3, 3),
        activation=activation_func,
        padding='same', strides=2),
    layers.BatchNormalization(),
    layers.Conv2D(16, (3, 3),
        activation=activation_func,
        padding='same', strides=2),
    layers.BatchNormalization(), ])

    self.decoder = tf.keras.Sequential([
        layers.Conv2DTranspose(16, (3, 3),
            activation=activation_func,
            padding='same', strides=2),
        layers.BatchNormalization(),
        layers.Conv2DTranspose(32, (3, 3),
        activation=activation_func,
        padding='same',strides=2),

    layers.BatchNormalization(),

    layers.Conv2DTranspose(64, (3, 3),
        activation=activation_func,
        padding='same', strides=2), layers.BatchNormalization(),
        layers.Conv2D(1, (3, 3),
            activation='sigmoid', padding='same'),
        layers.Cropping2D(cropping=((2, 2),(2, 2)))
    ])

def call(self, x):
    encoded = self.encoder(x)
    decoded = self.decoder(encoded)
    return decoded
```

This time we create a class in Python called `Denoise_Autoencoder`, the class is used to create a denoising autoencoder. The class inherits from the `tf.keras.Model`. This way the class can be behave like a Keras model.

The `init()` method of the class is used to initialize the class and allow it to use all the method from `keras.Model`.

Inside the `init()` method is the code to create the denoiser autoencoder. First you build the encoder, and like every type of autoencoder, you compress the input image in the latent dimension. In this code, the encoder is built using `tf.keras.Sequential`, which is a stack of layers group together and is used to build the neural network. Listing 6-9 shows the details of the call to create the encoder.

Listing 6-9. The Code Used to Create the Encoder Using tf.keras.Sequential

```
self.encoder = tf.keras.Sequential([
    layers.Input(shape=(28, 28, 1)),
        layers.Conv2D(64, (3, 3), activation='leaky_relu', padding='same',
        strides=2),
        layers.BatchNormalization(),
        layers.Conv2D(32, (3, 3), activation='leaky_relu', padding='same',
        strides=2),
        layers.BatchNormalization(),
        layers.Conv2D(16, (3, 3), activation='leaky_relu', padding='same',
        strides=2),
        layers.BatchNormalization(),
])
```

The encoder takes an input of 28x28 with one dimension, which is defined in `layers.Input`. This is essentially the dimension of the array in input that represents the image.

The first operation we do in the encoder is *convolution*, which is done using the `Conv2D` class in TensorFlow. This creates a convolution kernel that will be applied to the 2D dimension, the height and width of the images. The idea behind the convolution is to reduce the dimension of the image and apply a mathematical operation defined by the *kernel*; in this case we define a 3x3 kernel. A kernel is essentially a matrix with specific values used to highlight some specific characteristic in the image. For example, if you want to highlight a border or sharpen an image. The first parameter, 64, indicates the number of filters to apply. The activation function is LeakyReLU, which allows a small gradient if the input is negative. This condition can be happen when you apply a convolution operation to an image. To avoid missing important values in the data, the LeakyReLU activation is considered to be the best choice. Other important conditions for a convolution operation are the *stride* and the *padding*. In this case, with the value of stride=2, you essentially reduce the dimension of the matrix in half. This because we move the kernel, the matrix applied to the data, from left to right, moving it by two pixels at the time. Figure 6-6 shows an example of a kernel applied to an image.

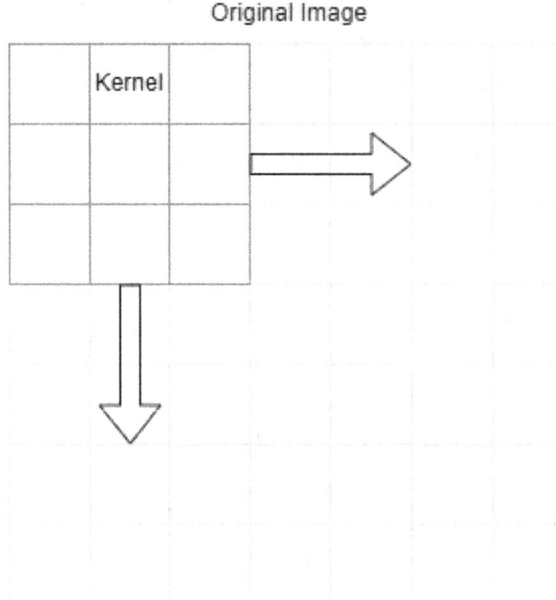

Figure 6-6. *A kernel applied to an image*

As you can see in the code, you have three different convolutional layers, and the size of the kernel is always half of the previous one. This is because you reduced in half the dimension of the input data. In the middle of the convolution layer is a batch normalization layer, which is used to stabilize the training of the neural network, because we "normalize" the data through rescaling and recentering the data.

If you are familiar with the other neural network, the encoder is similar to a CNN, but instead it's used to classify or recognize an image. CNNs usually reduce the image and learn the important features for reconstructing the data.

The decoder is built the same way, but in this case we execute the opposite operation of a convolution, the transpose, as you can see in Listing 6-10. The transpose is the mathematical opposite of the convolution.

Listing 6-10. The Decoder Function

```
self.decoder = tf.keras.Sequential([
    layers.Conv2DTranspose(16, (3, 3),
        activation=activation_func,
        padding='same',
        strides=2),
    layers.BatchNormalization(),
    layers.Conv2DTranspose(32, (3, 3),
        activation=activation_func,
        padding='same',
        strides=2),
    layers.BatchNormalization(),
    layers.Conv2DTranspose(64, (3, 3),
        activation=activation_func,
        padding='same',
        strides=2),
    layers.BatchNormalization(),
    layers.Conv2D(1, (3, 3),
        activation='sigmoid',
        padding='same'),
    layers.Cropping2D(cropping=((2, 2), (2, 2)))
])
```

In this case, you essentially start with a 16x16 image and use the transpose operation to rebuild it. The code applies a kernel with the same dimension but in this case it makes the data bigger. The last layer of the decoder is `Cropping2D`, which is because when the code rebuilt the image, it reached a dimension of 30x30. Because you wanted a 28x28 image, the code just cuts two pixels off for the final image.

Because this is a denoise autoencoder, you need to train it using a "noisy" image. In this case, you can do that simply by adding random noise to the image. Listing 6-11 shows how to do that. The code is very simple, you just define a noise factor, which indicates how much noise you want to add to the image, and then create a new noisy image. This will create a "noisy" image that will be used to train the autoencoder.

Listing 6-11. The Function for Adding Noise to the Image

```
def create_noisy_data(images, noise_factor=0.2):
    noisy_images = images + noise_factor * tf.random.
    normal(shape=images.shape)
    return tf.clip_by_value(noisy_images, clip_value_min=0.,
    clip_value_max=1.)
```

When you run the autoencoder, you will see a result like Figure 6-7, which shows the original image, the noisy image, and the reconstructed image. As you can see, the reconstructed image removes all the added noise and presents the image as cleanly as possible.

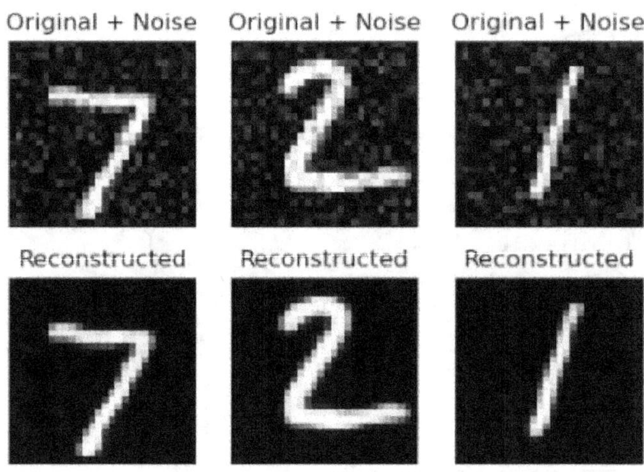

Figure 6-7. *The result of the Python denoise autoencoder*

You have now written the autoencoder in Python, so you're ready to see how to implement it in Julia.

Denoising Autoencoder with Julia

In Julia, you do the same operation as in Python. The Julia code to create the denoising autoencoder is shown in Listing 6-12.

Listing 6-12. The Denoising Autoencoder in Julia

```julia
function denoising_autoencoder()
    println("Building Denoising Autoencoder")

    encoder = Chain(
        Conv((3, 3), 1 => 64, leakyrelu, stride=2, pad=1),
        BatchNorm(64),
        Conv((3, 3), 64 => 32, leakyrelu, stride=2, pad=1),
        BatchNorm(32),
        Conv((3, 3), 32 => 16, leakyrelu, stride=2, pad=1),
        BatchNorm(16)
    )

    decoder = Chain(
        ConvTranspose((3, 3), 16 => 16, leakyrelu, stride=2, pad=1,
        outpad=1),
        BatchNorm(16),
        ConvTranspose((3, 3), 16 => 32, leakyrelu, stride=2, pad=1,
        outpad=1),
        BatchNorm(32),
        ConvTranspose((3, 3), 32 => 64, leakyrelu, stride=2, pad=1,
        outpad=1),
        BatchNorm(64),
        Conv((3, 3), 64 => 1, σ, pad=1)
    )

    return Chain(encoder, decoder)
end
```

In Julia you use the Chain function from the Flux library, which emulates what you
have with tf.keras.Sequential in Python. The concept is essentially the same—they
stack layers to create a neural network.

The encoder in Listing 6-13 performs the similar operation you saw in Python. It
executes a convolutional operation using a LeakyReLU and a stride for downsampling
the image. In particular, it cuts in half the dimension of the image at every single
operation. Between the convolutional operation is a BatchNorm layer, which executes a
batch normalization on the data. This speeds up the execution of the neural network.

At the end of the encoder, the image will have a size of 16x16 and this will be the input of the decoder. An important parameter is outpad=1, which ensures that the output dimensions are the same as indicated in the input.

Listing 6-13. The Encoder Write in Julia

```
encoder = Chain(
    Conv((3, 3), 1 => 64, leakyrelu, stride=2, pad=1),
    BatchNorm(64),
    Conv((3, 3), 64 => 32, leakyrelu, stride=2, pad=1),
    BatchNorm(32),
    Conv((3, 3), 32 => 16, leakyrelu, stride=2, pad=1),
    BatchNorm(16)
)
```

The parameters to extract the feature are indicated with the code 1 => 64, 64 => 32 and 32 => 16. This parameter essentially tells the Conv function to reduce the feature until you don't have the last layer, where we choose to learn the most important feature for the image. This features are essentially the *code*, or *latent space*, for the autoencoder.

The decoder, shown in Listing 6-14, starts with an input dimension of the image of 16x16 and uses the ConvTranspose function to upsample the image in order to rebuild the original data. In this case, the stride=2, is not used to cut the dimension of the image in half. It instead doubles the dimension, because you want to rebuild the original image, without the noise.

Listing 6-14. The Decoder Part in Julia

```
decoder = Chain(
    ConvTranspose((3, 3),
        16 => 16,
        leakyrelu,
        stride=2,
        pad=1,
        outpad=1),
    BatchNorm(16),
    ConvTranspose((3, 3),
        16 => 32,
```

```
        leakyrelu,
        stride=2,
        pad=1,
        outpad=1),
    BatchNorm(32),
    ConvTranspose((3, 3),
        32 => 64,
        leakyrelu,
        stride=2,
        pad=1,
        outpad=1),
    BatchNorm(64),
Conv((3, 3),
        64 => 1,
        σ,
        pad=1)
)
```

The outpad=1 parameter is used to ensure the output is what you expect, between the transpose layer we have the BatchNorm layer, which is used for the normalization of the data. The last layer of the decoder is a convolutional layer, which creates the Conv function of the Flux framework. This is used to re-create the image of the dimension you want. You move from the 64 to 1, which indicates the full image. The activation function in this case is a Sigmoid, and is indicated by the letter σ. The sigmoid is used to have value between 0 and 1, and the result of the image is a grayscale image.

It's important to note that the image will be 32x32, because the code upscales the image. But the original image is 28x28. If you compute the loss in this way you get an error, which is why you need to crop the image. This is done in the loss function as shown in Listing 6-15.

Listing 6-15. The Function Used to Compute the Loss in Julia

```
function compute_loss(autoencoder, noisy_x, clean_x)
    decoded = autoencoder(noisy_x)
    decoded = decoded[3:end-2, 3:end-2, :, :]
    return Flux.Losses.mse(decoded, clean_x)
end
```

The decoded=decoded[3:end-2,3:end-2,:,:] line will cut two dimensions—height and width—and will remove two pixels at the end of the two dimensions. This essentially translates the 32x32 image into a 28x28 image, which is the original dimensions. The denoiser autoencoder adds noise to the original image, which is shown in Listing 6-16.

Listing 6-16. The Julia Function to Add Noise in the Data

```julia
function add_noise(data, noise_level=0.1)
    noise = noise_level * randn(Float32, size(data))
    return clamp.(data + noise, 0.0, 1.0)
end
```

This code essentially adds some random Gaussian noise to the data. The level of the noise is 0.1. We choose this value, but we can have even more noise. In this case it will be more complex for the autoencoder to learn the original data, but at the same time it can make the autoencoder more resistant to the noise.

The noise=noise_level*randn(Float32,size(data)) line is used to create the random noise that will be added to the data. The noise is sampled from the normal distribution, which means that we add noise but based on the real data. The random value generated is multiplied by the noise level defined, in this case 0.1, which gives the measure of the noise that will be added to the image.

The function will return a clamp of the data with the added noise. This operation creates a value between 0 and 1, which is used to have some normalized data and not allow for negative data. If the value of the data plus the noise is less than 0, the clamp will put the value at 0. On the other hand, if the value is more than 1, the clamp will put the value to 1. This operation prevents having data that preserves the integrity of the data.

Conclusion

This chapter explained how autoencoders are used and the differences between autoencoders and GANs. You saw in particular two types of autoencoders—the sparse autoencoder and the denoising autoencoder. There are other types of autoencoders as well, like the contractive autoencoder and the undercomplete autoencoder. Another type is the convolutional autoencoder, and you essentially write one when you design the denoising autoencoder. The different types of autoencoders are connected to the loss function. For the sparse autoencoder, for example, you add sparsity to the data, which pushes the autoencoder to learn only the important features and the loss function to penalize the data that is far from the original data.

Another important lesson you learned is that the encoder and the decoder can have every type of neural network. The denoising autoencoder used a CNN to encode the data, but in this case we didn't use the CNN to classify but to learn the features of the data and to better reconstruct the data. Using the denoising autoencoder, you can rebuild or reconstruct images from other types of data. This is important in many fields of application. Imagine for example you need to reconstruct an image captured from an x-ray or from other important medical examinations. This shows the real power of deep generative artificial intelligence. It has not only the capacity to build text and create audio, but it can also rebuild and reconstruct images or other forms of data. This capacity can be used in a wide range of applications, from cybersecurity to financial applications.

In the next chapter, you learn about another type of autoencoder, the variational autoencoder.

## CHAPTER 7

Variational Autoencoders

In this chapter, you learn about another revolutionary deep learning architecture, the variational autoencoder. Variational autoencoders (VAEs) are similar to autoencoders and GANs, learning the *latent variables* of the data to understand how to represent and create new data. Variational autoencoders have gained popularity in recent years due to their ability to describe observations in a probabilistic manner. This ability makes variational autoencoders able to be employed in a wide range of applications, for example, generating audio, video or text; anomaly detection; and denoising; just to name a few. In this chapter, you learn the theory behind the variational autoencoders and implement some examples using Julia and Python.

How Variational Autoencoders (VAEs) Work

A variational autoencoder (VAE) is a type of generative deep learning architecture that learns the probability distribution of complex data, such as images, audio, or text. In a variational autoencoder, unlike an autoencoder, the encoders will map the input data to the mean and variance of a probability distribution in a compressed *latent space*. This allows the encoder to sample and create new data coherent with the input data. The decoder will then reconstruct the data from the sampled latent vector. The idea behind the variational autoencoder is to learn the probability distribution over the latent variables. This probability distribution will be used to generate new data in the output that has the same probability distribution as the original data. Similar to autoencoders, variational autoencoders can generate new data that is similar to the original data, but because of the probability distribution, the data is not the same. This capability make the variational autoencoder more effective in tasks like image and audio generation, and in general, all tasks that require a probabilistic variation of the original data. The variational autoencoder learns the probability distribution using the *variational inference*.

© Pierluigi Riti 2026
P. Riti, *Introduction to Generative AI with Julia and Python*, https://doi.org/10.1007/979-8-8688-2329-9_7

Variational inference is a machine learning technique that transforms an intractable inference problem into an optimization problem. The goal of the variational inference is to approximate the conditional density of the latent variables given observed variables.

The variational inference works by defining a simpler, parameterized family of distributions and finding the member that is closest to the complex posterior. Typically, this is calculated using a Kullback-Leibler divergence to measure the closeness. Variational inference is faster than traditional methods like the Markov Chain Monte Carlo sampling, which makes the variational inference more suitable for large datasets.

The reason behind the efficiency of the variational inference is that, with the variational inference, instead of sampling directly from a distribution, the variational inference transforms the problem into an optimization problem. With the problem transformed into an optimization problem, you can now use different techniques to solve it, like gradient descent. In addition, variational inference is very effective in a wide range of applications, and because of its capacity to work with large datasets, it shows better performance with natural language processing and computer vision.

The Importance of Latent Space

Latent space is an important concept to understand variational autoencoders. In the *latent space,* we can find latent variables, which represent the fundamental structure and characteristics of the data. This variable can be thought of as a comprehensive representation of the data that maintains the most crucial aspects of the data itself.

In a variational autoencoder, latent variables are the parameters learned, which can be used to define the data distribution from which you start to generate the new data. The latent variables capture the statistical aspect of the data—the mean and the variance.

When you think of the latent variables, you need to think of a set of *continuous variables*, because a continuous variable is a desirable property for many tasks. A continuous variable means that small changes in the latent variables result in minor changes in the generated output. By design, a variational autoencoder enforces a smooth, continuous latent space, and this makes it an excellent choice for all tasks that require the generation of new, realistic data.

Another important aspect of variational autoencoders belongs to the family of what we call Bayesian deep learning, which is because the variational inference is based on the Bayesian methodologies. The variational inference is an approximate Bayesian inference method. Bayesian methods provide a framework for reasoning about the uncertainty in the parameters of the model. This is an important consideration when you're learning representation in an unsupervised manner.

The Variational Autoencoder Architecture

Variational autoencoders share a similar architecture to autoencoders. Figure 7-1 shows the architecture.

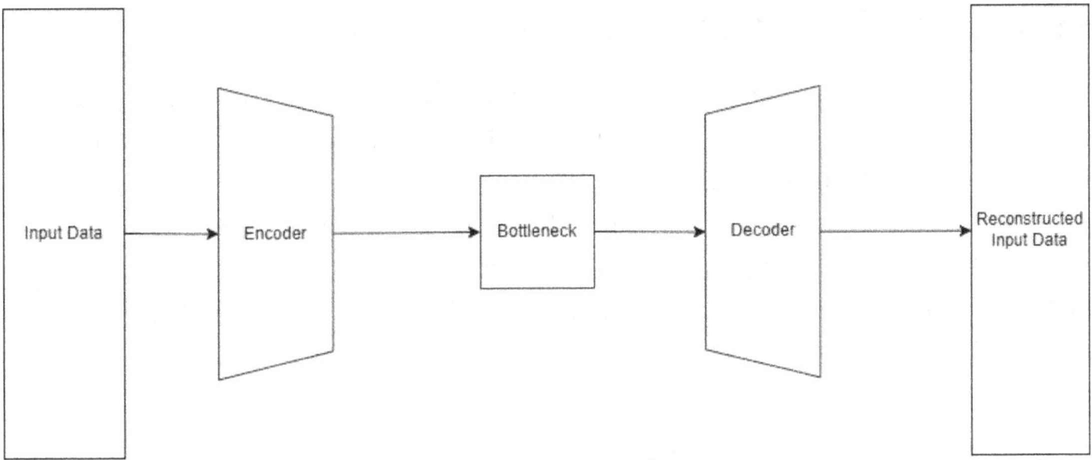

Figure 7-1. *The variational autoencoder architecture*

As you can see, variational autoencoders and autoencoders have an encoder and decoder and have a bottleneck layer that's used to select the most important features to represent the data. The difference between the variational autoencoder and the autoencoder is how they select the features. Variational autoencoders use the mean and the variance of the data. Variational autoencoders are very flexible for processing and generating new data, and because of that, you can define variation on the main architecture. The next sections describe some variations of the main architecture. In particular, they describe:

- Convolutional variational autoencoders

- Recurrent variational autoencoders

Convolutional Variational Autoencoders

Convolutional variational autoencoders are particularly useful when you work with images. This type of architecture can be used when you need to generate new data starting with the image.

In this type of architecture, you use a CNN for both the encoder and the decoder layer of the network, which makes the architecture useful when you need to work with images.

Recurrent Variational Autoencoders

Recurrent variational autoencoders are a type of variational autoencoder used to work with recurrent data, which makes this type of variational autoencoder the perfect choice for working with NLP tasks or with any temporal data.

In a recurrent variational autoencoder, the encoder and decoder introduce some recurrent layers, such as long short-term memory (LSTM). This is the same layer used on the transformer, and it allows the neural network to "remember" data that can be used to better understand the data to generate.

Examples of Variational Autoencoders

As with every other architecture discussed in this book, it's time to get our hands dirty and implement some basic variational autoencoders. The first type you will implement is a convolutional variational autoencoder. You will also implement a denoising variational autoencoder. You'll first create an implementation in Python and then one in Julia.

The Convolutional Variational Autoencoder in Python

The convolutional variational autoencoder can be used to replicate the MINST dataset.

Before I show you the code, you need to understand some important concepts that we will coding in the convolutional variational autoencoder. In this implementation, you will encounter three important components:

- The sampling layer

- The encoder

- The decoder

The *sampling layer* is the first key component of the convolutional variational autoencoder. This layer is responsible for the *reparameterization trick.* This technique is used in the VAEs to enable the backpropagation through stochastic sampling. Using this technique is essential to be able to train the VAE using a gradient based optimization technique.

The reparameterization trick is needed in a VAEs because of the nature of the VAE itself. In the VAEs, the *encoder* predicts the mean and the standard deviation of a latent Gaussian distribution. The data is then generated performing a stochastic sample. Generating data in this way introduces some randomness, which makes the data non-differentiable. If you want to use a gradient-based optimization technique, the data must be differentiable and this where the reparameterization trick comes in. This trick make the data differentiable, because it separates the stochastic data from the learned date, which allows the gradient flow during the backpropagation.

The sampling process is rewritten to make it differentiable. You don't directly calculate the Gaussian distribution, known also as a *normal distribution,* $Z \sim N(0, 1)$ but instead reprocess the formula to enable the reparameterization trick: $Z = \mu + \sigma \cdot \in$. Where:

- μ is the *mean* of the data

- σ is the *standard deviation* of the data

- $\in$ is a *noise term* sampled from the a standard normal distribution $\in \sim N(0, 1)$

The reformulation ensures that the randomness will be isolated in $\in$, which is independent of the model parameters. Isolating the randomness make the model parameters μ and σ part of a deterministic function, which makes them differentiable. The sampling layer, shown in Listing 7-1, introduces the `import` needed and the variable used in the rest of the code.

Listing 7-1. The Sampling Function of the Convolutional Variational Autoencoder

```
import tensorflow as tf
from tensorflow import keras
from tensorflow.keras import layers
import numpy as np
import matplotlib.pyplot as plt
```

```
# --- Configuration ---
# Set the dimensionality of the latent space.
LATENT_DIM = 32
IMAGE_SHAPE = (28, 28, 1)
BATCH_SIZE = 128
# Increased epochs for better convergence
EPOCHS = 30
# Beta value: controls the weight of the KL divergence loss (lower beta ->
better reconstruction)
BETA = 0.5

class Sampling(layers.Layer):
    def call(self, inputs):
        z_mean, z_log_var = inputs
        batch = tf.shape(z_mean)[0]
        dim = tf.shape(z_mean)[1]
        epsilon = tf.keras.backend.random_normal(shape=(batch, dim))
        return z_mean + tf.exp(0.5 * z_log_var) * epsilon
```

In this case, you create a new class and use a Keras layer to make the class a custom trainable part of the model graph.

z_mean and z_log_var are two input tensor parameters that come in from the previous layer, which is normally the dense layer of the encoder. z_mean represents μ, which is the mean vector of the Latent Gaussian Distribution. z_log_var represents the $\log(\sigma^2)$, which is the log variance of the variance vector. We use the log for better numerical stabilization during the optimization.

Right after the calculation of the mean and the variance, the code extracts the dimension of the batch and the dimension. This is done with batch and dim and defines the shape of the random noise vector used to generate the data.

At this point, you need to create a random noise vector, which will represent the $\in$ and will be calculated using a random normal distribution, with the shape previously identified in this line of code:

```
epsilon = tf.keras.backend.random_normal(shape=(batch, dim))
```

With all the basics calculated, you can now code the reparameterization trick. This is done directly in the return of the Python class. Epsilon stabilizes the training. When you calculate the sampling, you return the exponential using a value of 0.5, which can lead to numerical instability. To stabilize the value, you calculate the Epsilon, and this will correct for any numerical instability.

The next crucial component is the encoder, which is used to get the input data—in this case, the MNIST images—and produce the parameters for the latent distribution, which are the mean and the log variance. The code for the encoder is shown in Listing 7-2.

Listing 7-2. The Encoder Network

```python
def build_encoder(input_shape, latent_dim):
    encoder_inputs = keras.Input(shape=input_shape)

    # Convolutional layers
    x = layers.Conv2D(64, 3, activation="relu", strides=2, padding="same")
    (encoder_inputs)
    x = layers.Conv2D(64, 3, activation="relu", strides=2,
    padding="same")(x)

    x = layers.Flatten()(x)

    # Bottleneck layers
    x = layers.Dense(64, activation="relu")(x)

    # Output layers for mean (z_mean) and log-variance (z_log_var)
    z_mean = layers.Dense(latent_dim, name="z_mean")(x)
    z_log_var = layers.Dense(latent_dim, name="z_log_var")(x)

    # Sampling layer for the actual latent vector z
    z = Sampling()([z_mean, z_log_var])

    return keras.Model(encoder_inputs, [z_mean, z_log_var, z],
    name="encoder")
```

The encoder will break down the image into its probabilistic representation of the latent space, which will be used to rebuild the image.

Because we are developing a convolutional variational autoencoder, the first layer will be a convolutional layer. This is created with some basic parameters. 64 is the number of filters extracted, this is the feature maps. For the convolutional operation, we use a kernel size of 3, which will create 3x3 windows. The *stride* of 2 will essentially reduce the image in half, from 28x28, the MNIST image, to 14x14. After the first convolutional layer, you execute a new convolutional layer, which is used to reduce the image map again. The parameters are the same as the first level of *downsampling*. In this case, you move from a 14x14 image to a 7x7 image, which will represent the deepest representation of the image in a two-dimensional vector.

Before you can send the code to a dense layer, you need to flatten the data from a 2D vector to 1D vector. To do that, you use this line of code `x = layers.Flatten()(x)`, which will transform the input into a 1D vector. At this point, you are ready to feed the dense layer, which represents the bottleneck layer for the VAE. This is done with the line `x = layers.Dense(64, activation="relu")(x)`. With the dense layer created, you can start to calculate the mean and the log variation of the data. Both are calculated on the dense layer with the most important feature of the image.

The mean, μ, is calculated using `z_mean = layers.Dense(latent_dim, name="z_mean")(x)`, which provides the mean of the latent dimension vector. The log variance is calculated using `z_log_var = layers.Dense(latent_dim, name="z_log_var")(x)`.

With the mean and log variation now calculated, you can call the sampling layer, which is done by the encoder with this line of code `z = Sampling()([z_mean, z_log_var])`. This code creates the final model for the encoder. The line of code used to do that is `keras.Model(encoder_inputs, [z_mean, z_log_var, z], name="encoder")`.

The line will return a Keras model that maps the input image into three different latent spaces, which are the mean, μ, the log variance, $\log(\sigma^2)$, and the latent code, Z.

With the encoder defined, you can now define the decoder. The goal of the decoder is to generate a new image starting from the encoded latent code. The decoder layer is where the new data is *generated*. The decoder will generate the data and perform the mapping of the latent code Z to generate the image X. Mathematically we can define this operation in this way: $P(X|Z)$. This is achieved by reversing the downsampling and the convolutional operation made by the encoder. Listing 7-3 shows the code for the decoder.

Listing 7-3. The Decoder Network Used on the Convolutional Variational Autoencoder

```python
def build_decoder(latent_dim):
    decoder_inputs = keras.Input(shape=(latent_dim,))

    # Start with a Dense layer to get back to the 7x7 bottleneck shape (7
    * 7 * 64)
    x = layers.Dense(7 * 7 * 64, activation="relu")(decoder_inputs)
    x = layers.Reshape((7, 7, 64))(x)

    # Deconvolutional/Transpose layers for upsampling
    # 7x7 -> 14x14
    x = layers.Conv2DTranspose(64, 3, activation="relu", strides=2,
    padding="same")(x)
    # 14x14 -> 28x28 (Final image size)
    x = layers.Conv2DTranspose(32, 3, activation="relu", strides=2,
    padding="same")(x)

    # Output layer with sigmoid activation for pixel values between 0 and 1
    decoder_outputs = layers.Conv2DTranspose(
        1, 3, activation="sigmoid", padding="same"
    )(x)

    return keras.Model(decoder_inputs, decoder_outputs, name="decoder")
```

As you can see, the decoder starts with a dense layer in order to scale up the size of the data, followed by two layers of Conv2DTranspose. This layer executes a transpose operation, which is essentially the opposite of a convolution operation. The layers are used to upgrade the size of the vector, and the vector will be upgraded with the newly generated data. The layer continues upscaling the size of the data until you define the last layer of transpose. The model will then return the output as newly generated images.

Building the Variational Autoencoder

With all the components now defined, you can start to build the variational autoencoder, as presented in Listing 7-4.

Listing 7-4. The Code for the Variational Autoencoder

```python
class VAE(keras.Model):
    # Added beta parameter to control KL loss weight
    def __init__(self, encoder, decoder, beta=1.0, **kwargs):
        super().__init__(**kwargs)
        self.encoder = encoder
        self.decoder = decoder
        self.beta = beta # Store beta factor

        # Define metrics to track losses
        self.total_loss_tracker = keras.metrics.Mean(name="total_loss")
        self.reconstruction_loss_tracker = keras.metrics.Mean(
            name="reconstruction_loss"
        )
        self.kl_loss_tracker = keras.metrics.Mean(name="kl_loss")

    # Property to expose the metrics
    @property
    def metrics(self):
        return [
            self.total_loss_tracker,
            self.reconstruction_loss_tracker,
            self.kl_loss_tracker,
        ]

    # Custom training step that incorporates the VAE loss components
    def train_step(self, data):
        # We assume the data is (x_train, ) where x_train is the
        # input image
        x = data

        with tf.GradientTape() as tape:
            # 1. Forward Pass
            z_mean, z_log_var, z = self.encoder(x)
            reconstruction = self.decoder(z)
```

```python
        # 2. Reconstruction Loss (Binary Cross-Entropy for
        binarized images)
        # The shapes are now guaranteed to match (None, 28, 28, 1)
        reconstruction_loss = tf.reduce_mean(
            tf.reduce_sum(
                keras.losses.binary_crossentropy(x, reconstruction),
                axis=(1, 2) # Summing over H and W dimensions
            )
        )

        # 3. KL Divergence Loss
        # KL divergence between q(z|x) and P(z) (standard normal)
        # Formula: -0.5 * sum(1 + log(sigma^2) - mu^2 - sigma^2)
        kl_loss = -0.5 * (1 + z_log_var - tf.square(z_mean) - tf.exp(z_
        log_var))
        kl_loss = tf.reduce_mean(tf.reduce_sum(kl_loss, axis=1))
        # Summing over latent dimension

        # 4. Total Loss (Applying Beta)
        total_loss = reconstruction_loss + self.beta * kl_loss # Apply
        the beta factor

    # Apply gradients
    grads = tape.gradient(total_loss, self.trainable_weights)
    self.optimizer.apply_gradients(zip(grads, self.trainable_weights))

    # Update metrics
    self.total_loss_tracker.update_state(total_loss)
    self.reconstruction_loss_tracker.update_state(reconstruction_loss)
    self.kl_loss_tracker.update_state(kl_loss)

    return {
        "loss": self.total_loss_tracker.result(),
        "reconstruction_loss": self.reconstruction_loss_tracker.
        result(),
        "kl_loss": self.kl_loss_tracker.result(),
    }
```

This example uses a MNIST image because the code uses Binary Cross Entropy, which works with a binary image, a black and white image like the one in the MNIST data. If you have a full-color image, it's better to use mean-squared error or categorical_crossentropy. The choice is connected to the type of image you need to reproduce. If, for example you work with different images that need to be categorized, categorical_crossentropy is the perfect choice. Mean-squared error is better when the decoder needs to produce a continuous output distribution, which means that you will reconstruct only one type of image.

With all the main components defined, it's time to build the variational autoencoder. This code will override the Keras.Model class, because you want to use the fit() method but want to override some internal methods.

Because you have now a class, you use the __init__ method to initialize and define the encoder and the decoder. We use a Beta factor of 1.0, which represents the weight of the Kullback-Leibler (KL) divergence loss.

In the init, we define some metrics used to calculate the loss function. This is necessary because we override the Keras metrics. The @property decorator redefines which metrics are calculated when you call the fit() command. In this case, you will see:

- Loss tracker metrics

- Reconstruction loss tracker metrics

- KL loss metrics

This metric is specific to your class and is overridden. Another functionality you will override are the *training steps,* which are defined in this code:

```
def train_step(self, data):
    # We assume the data is (x_train, ) where x_train is the input image
    x = data

    with tf.GradientTape() as tape:
        # 1. Forward Pass
        z_mean, z_log_var, z = self.encoder(x)
        reconstruction = self.decoder(z)

        # 2. Reconstruction Loss (Binary Cross-Entropy for
        binarized images)
```

```
# The shapes are now guaranteed to match (None, 28, 28, 1)
    reconstruction_loss = tf.reduce_mean(
        tf.reduce_sum(
            keras.losses.binary_crossentropy(x, reconstruction),
            axis=(1, 2) # Summing over H and W dimensions
        )
    )
```

This code is specialized for the loss function, `tf.GradientTape()`, which is used to calculate the forward pass for the backpropagation. It will use the mean and the log variation from the encoder to calculate the loss from the reconstructed data. The last step is the reconstruction loss. Because you have a gray image, you can use a Binary Cross Entropy, and it's calculated on the reconstructed image. This is done because you want to understand how different the image produced by the decoder is from the input one.

At this point, you have all the components ready and just need to train the network with some sample data. This is essentially similar to what you did in other architectures so I do not review it again. When you run the code, you will see a result similar to Figure 7-2.

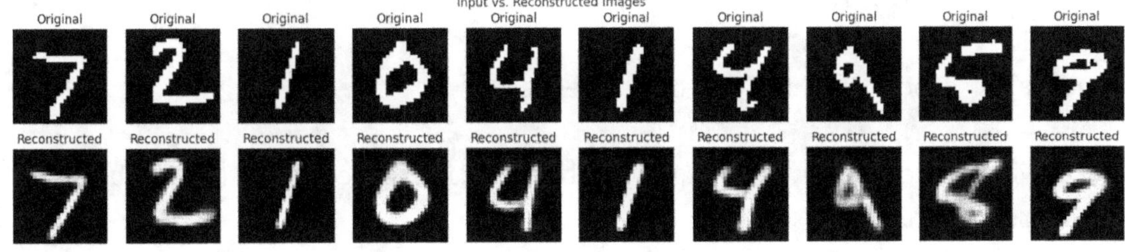

Figure 7-2. *The result of the convolutional autoencoder*

As you can see, the image is very well reconstructed. This make the variational autoencoder one of the best architectures for this type of exercise. Next, you see a small variation of the variational autoencoder, the denoising variational autoencoder.

The Denoising Variational Autoencoder

A denoising variational autoencoder is a type of variational autoencoder that's used to remove the noise from the original data.

To develop these types of VAEs, you train on noisy data. You create noisy data by adding random noisy data to the original image, and then letting the VAE clean the data. This allows the encoder to map the noisy data into the latent space, where the decoder will learn the mean variance of the data without the noise. The changes to the previous code are minimal. In particular, you need to add a *noisy factor* to add noise to the original image. The encoder and decoder remain the same. Another change is in the VAE class that will be trained with the noise data. This can then learn how to rebuild the image removing the noise. The code is shown in Listing 7-5.

Listing 7-5. The Denoising Variational Autoencoder

```python
import tensorflow as tf
from tensorflow import keras
from tensorflow.keras import layers
import numpy as np
import matplotlib.pyplot as plt

# --- Configuration ---
# Set the dimensionality of the latent space.
LATENT_DIM = 32
IMAGE_SHAPE = (28, 28, 1)
BATCH_SIZE = 128
# Increased epochs for better convergence
EPOCHS = 30
# Beta value: controls the weight of the KL divergence loss (lower beta ->
better reconstruction)
BETA = 0.5
# NOISE FACTOR: Standard deviation of Gaussian noise added to the
input images
NOISE_FACTOR = 0.5

# 1. Reparameterization Trick Sampling Layer
# This custom layer implements the reparameterization trick:
# z = z_mean + exp(0.5 * z_log_var) * epsilon
class Sampling(layers.Layer):
    """Uses (z_mean, z_log_var) to sample z, the vector encoding a
    digit."""
```

```python
    def call(self, inputs):
        z_mean, z_log_var = inputs
        batch = tf.shape(z_mean)[0]
        dim = tf.shape(z_mean)[1]

        # Draw epsilon from a standard normal distribution
        epsilon = tf.keras.backend.random_normal(shape=(batch, dim))

        # Calculate z
        return z_mean + tf.exp(0.5 * z_log_var) * epsilon

# 2. Define the Encoder Network
def build_encoder(input_shape, latent_dim):
    encoder_inputs = keras.Input(shape=input_shape)

    # Convolutional layers
    # 28x28 -> 14x14
    x = layers.Conv2D(64, 3, activation="relu", strides=2, padding="same")
    (encoder_inputs)
    # 14x14 -> 7x7 (Bottleneck size)
    x = layers.Conv2D(64, 3, activation="relu", strides=2,
    padding="same")(x)

    x = layers.Flatten()(x)

    # Bottleneck layers
    x = layers.Dense(64, activation="relu")(x)

    # Output layers for mean (z_mean) and log-variance (z_log_var)
    z_mean = layers.Dense(latent_dim, name="z_mean")(x)
    z_log_var = layers.Dense(latent_dim, name="z_log_var")(x)

    # Sampling layer for the actual latent vector z
    z = Sampling()([z_mean, z_log_var])

    return keras.Model(encoder_inputs, [z_mean, z_log_var, z],
    name="encoder")
```

```python
# 3. Define the Decoder Network
def build_decoder(latent_dim):
    decoder_inputs = keras.Input(shape=(latent_dim,))

    # Start with a Dense layer to get back to the 7x7 bottleneck shape (7
    * 7 * 64)
    x = layers.Dense(7 * 7 * 64, activation="relu")(decoder_inputs)
    x = layers.Reshape((7, 7, 64))(x)

    # Deconvolutional/Transpose layers for upsampling
    # 7x7 -> 14x14
    x = layers.Conv2DTranspose(64, 3, activation="relu", strides=2,
    padding="same")(x)
    # 14x14 -> 28x28 (Final image size)
    x = layers.Conv2DTranspose(32, 3, activation="relu", strides=2,
    padding="same")(x)

    # Output layer with sigmoid activation for pixel values between 0 and 1
    decoder_outputs = layers.Conv2DTranspose(
        1, 3, activation="sigmoid", padding="same"
    )(x)

    return keras.Model(decoder_inputs, decoder_outputs, name="decoder")

# 4. Define the Denoising VAE Model with Custom Training Step
class VAE(keras.Model):
    # Added beta parameter to control KL loss weight
    def __init__(self, encoder, decoder, beta=1.0, **kwargs):
        super().__init__(**kwargs)
        self.encoder = encoder
        self.decoder = decoder
        self.beta = beta # Store beta factor

        # Define metrics to track losses
        self.total_loss_tracker = keras.metrics.Mean(name="total_loss")
        self.reconstruction_loss_tracker = keras.metrics.Mean(
            name="reconstruction_loss"
        )
        self.kl_loss_tracker = keras.metrics.Mean(name="kl_loss")
```

```python
# Property to expose the metrics
@property
def metrics(self):
    return [
        self.total_loss_tracker,
        self.reconstruction_loss_tracker,
        self.kl_loss_tracker,
    ]

# Custom training step that incorporates the VAE loss components
def train_step(self, data):
    # Data is a tuple (x_noisy, x_clean) provided via model.fit(x, y)
    x_noisy, x_clean = data

    with tf.GradientTape() as tape:
        # 1. Forward Pass: Encode the NOISY input
        z_mean, z_log_var, z = self.encoder(x_noisy)
        reconstruction = self.decoder(z)

        # 2. Reconstruction Loss: Compare RECONSTRUCTION vs
        CLEAN target
        # Using Binary Cross-Entropy, suitable for pixel values
        in [0, 1]
        reconstruction_loss = tf.reduce_mean(
            tf.reduce_sum(
                # CRUCIAL: Compare reconstruction to the CLEAN target
                (x_clean)
                keras.losses.binary_crossentropy(x_clean,
                reconstruction),
                axis=(1, 2) # Summing over H and W dimensions
            )
        )

        # 3. KL Divergence Loss (Same as standard VAE)
        kl_loss = -0.5 * (1 + z_log_var - tf.square(z_mean) - tf.exp(z_
        log_var))
        kl_loss = tf.reduce_mean(tf.reduce_sum(kl_loss, axis=1))
```

```
        # 4. Total Loss (Applying Beta)
        total_loss = reconstruction_loss + self.beta * kl_loss

    # Apply gradients
    grads = tape.gradient(total_loss, self.trainable_weights)
    self.optimizer.apply_gradients(zip(grads, self.trainable_weights))

    # Update metrics
    self.total_loss_tracker.update_state(total_loss)
    self.reconstruction_loss_tracker.update_state(reconstruction_loss)
    self.kl_loss_tracker.update_state(kl_loss)

    return {
        "loss": self.total_loss_tracker.result(),
        "reconstruction_loss": self.reconstruction_loss_tracker.
        result(),
        "kl_loss": self.kl_loss_tracker.result(),
    }

# 5. Data Preparation (Using MNIST for demonstration)
def load_and_prepare_data():
    (x_train, _), (x_test, _) = keras.datasets.mnist.load_data()

    # Reshape and normalize to [0, 1] (Continuous data for better
    denoising)
    x_train_clean = x_train.astype("float32") / 255.0
    x_test_clean = x_test.astype("float32") / 255.0

    # Add a channel dimension: (N, 28, 28) -> (N, 28, 28, 1)
    x_train_clean = np.expand_dims(x_train_clean, -1)
    x_test_clean = np.expand_dims(x_test_clean, -1)

    # ------------------ NOISING STEP ------------------
    # Create noisy versions by adding Gaussian noise scaled by NOISE_FACTOR
    noise_train = NOISE_FACTOR * np.random.normal(loc=0.0, scale=1.0,
    size=x_train_clean.shape)
    noise_test = NOISE_FACTOR * np.random.normal(loc=0.0, scale=1.0,
    size=x_test_clean.shape)
```

```python
    x_train_noisy = x_train_clean + noise_train
    x_test_noisy = x_test_clean + noise_test

    # Clip to keep values in the valid range [0, 1]
    x_train_noisy = np.clip(x_train_noisy, 0., 1.)
    x_test_noisy = np.clip(x_test_noisy, 0., 1.)

    # For DVAE, we return (noisy_input, clean_target)
    print(f"Training data shapes (Noisy Input / Clean Target): {x_train_
noisy.shape} / {x_train_clean.shape}")

    return (x_train_noisy, x_train_clean), (x_test_noisy, x_test_clean)

# 6. Generation Function for Visualization
def plot_results(models, data, batch_size=128, model_name="dvae_mnist"):
    encoder, decoder = models
    # Data is now a tuple: (x_test_noisy, x_test_clean)
    x_test_noisy, x_test_clean = data

    # 1. Visualize reconstruction/denoising
    x_test_noisy_subset = x_test_noisy[:BATCH_SIZE]
    x_test_clean_subset = x_test_clean[:BATCH_SIZE]

    # Encode NOISY data
    _, _, z_test = encoder.predict(x_test_noisy_subset, batch_
size=batch_size)
    # Decode to get RECONSTRUCTION/DENOISED output
    x_decoded = decoder.predict(z_test, batch_size=batch_size)

    # Plotting should show three rows: Clean Original, Noisy Input,
Denoised Output
    n = 10  # How many digits we will display
    plt.figure(figsize=(20, 6))
    for i in range(n):
        # Display Clean Original (Row 1)
        ax = plt.subplot(3, n, i + 1)
        plt.imshow(x_test_clean_subset[i].reshape(28, 28), cmap="gray")
        plt.title("Clean Original")
        ax.get_xaxis().set_visible(False)
```

```python
ax.get_yaxis().set_visible(False)

# Display Noisy Input (Row 2)
ax = plt.subplot(3, n, i + 1 + n)
plt.imshow(x_test_noisy_subset[i].reshape(28, 28), cmap="gray")
plt.title("Noisy Input")
ax.get_xaxis().set_visible(False)
ax.get_yaxis().set_visible(False)

# Display Denoised Output (Row 3)
ax = plt.subplot(3, n, i + 1 + 2 * n)
plt.imshow(x_decoded[i].reshape(28, 28), cmap="gray")
plt.title("Denoised Output")
ax.get_xaxis().set_visible(False)
ax.get_yaxis().set_visible(False)

plt.suptitle("Denoising VAE Results: Clean Original, Noisy Input, and
Denoised Output")
plt.show()

# 2. Visualize latent space (2D for LATENT_DIM=2)
# This block will only run if LATENT_DIM is explicitly set back to 2.
if LATENT_DIM == 2:
    # Re-run prediction on full test set for better latent space plot
    (x_test_full, y_test_full), (_, _) = keras.datasets.mnist.
    load_data()
    x_test_full = np.expand_dims(x_test_full.astype("float32") /
    255.0, -1)

    # Get the mean of the latent vector from the CLEAN data (or noisy
    if preferred)
    z_mean, _, _ = encoder.predict(x_test_full, batch_size=batch_size)

    plt.figure(figsize=(10, 10))
    plt.scatter(z_mean[:, 0], z_mean[:, 1], c=y_test_full, cmap='hsv',
    alpha=0.7)
    plt.colorbar()
    plt.xlabel("z[0] (Latent Dimension 1)")
```

```python
        plt.ylabel("z[1] (Latent Dimension 2)")
        plt.title("2D Latent Space Visualization (Color-coded by Digit)")
        plt.show()

# --- Main Execution ---
if __name__ == "__main__":

    # 1. Build components
    encoder = build_encoder(IMAGE_SHAPE, LATENT_DIM)
    decoder = build_decoder(LATENT_DIM)
    vae = VAE(encoder, decoder, beta=BETA)

    # 2. Compile VAE
    vae.compile(optimizer=keras.optimizers.Adam(learning_rate=1e-3))

    # 3. Prepare data: returns (noisy_input, clean_target)
    (x_train_noisy, x_train_clean), (x_test_noisy, x_test_clean) = load_
    and_prepare_data()

    # 4. Train the DVAE
    print("\n--- Starting DVAE Training ---")
    # Pass noisy data as X and clean data as Y (target)
    vae.fit(x=x_train_noisy, y=x_train_clean, epochs=EPOCHS, batch_
    size=BATCH_SIZE)
    print("--- Training Complete ---")

    # 5. Evaluate and Visualize
    # Pass both noisy input and clean target data for visualization
    plot_results((encoder, decoder), (x_test_noisy, x_test_clean),
    BATCH_SIZE)

    # 6. Generate new images from random latent points (Generative
    capability check)
    print("\n--- Generating New Samples from Latent Space ---")

    random_latent_vectors = tf.random.normal(shape=(25, LATENT_DIM))
    generated_images = decoder.predict(random_latent_vectors)

    plt.figure(figsize=(10, 10))
    for i in range(25):
```

```
    plt.subplot(5, 5, i + 1)
    plt.imshow(generated_images[i].reshape(28, 28), cmap="gray")
    plt.axis("off")
plt.suptitle("Generated Images from Random Latent Samples")
plt.show()
```

When we run this code, we will have a result similar to the one show in Figure 7-3, we see the original image, the one with the noise, and then the reconstructed one. The reconstructed image loss a little bit of their quality, this because in case of denoising we need to update some hyperparameter, but this will improve the training time, if you like, you can play with the parameter and see what will be better quality, you can improve the number of epoch, in our example I use 30 epoch, or reduce the beta, I really invite you to explore and see what suite better.

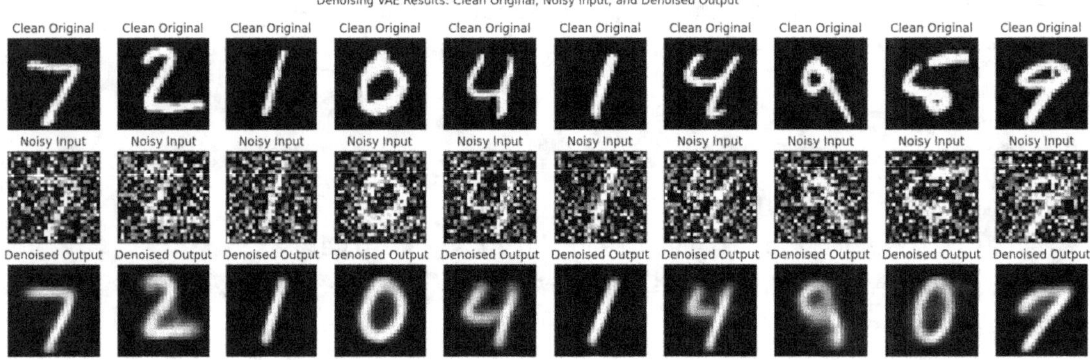

Figure 7-3. *The result of the denoising variational autoencoder*

Denoising Variational Autoencoder are particularly useful when we want to restore image or remove noise from the data. Like every other architecture let's see now how to code the same type of Variational Autoencoder using Julia.

The Convolutional Variational Autoencoder in Julia

The Julia implementation of the convolutional variational autoencoder is done using the Flux framework. This is the best deep learning library to use with Julia. The full code is shown in Listing 7-6. Let's analyze the main components and see how they are implemented in Julia.

Listing 7-6. The Julia Implementation of the Convolutional Variational Autoencoder

```julia
using Flux
using Flux: train!, mse, logitbinarycrossentropy
using MLDatasets
using Statistics: mean
using Random
using Printf
using Plots # <-- NEW: Added Plots.jl for visualization

# --- Configuration ---
const LATENT_DIM = 10     # Dimensionality of the latent space
const IMAGE_SIZE = 28 * 28  # 784 for MNIST (28x28)
const HIDDEN_DIM = 256    # Size of the intermediate dense layers
const EPOCHS = 20
const BATCH_SIZE = 128
const LEARNING_RATE = 0.001
const BETA = 1.0 # Weight for KL divergence (Beta-VAE concept)

# --- 1. Data Preparation ---

function load_and_preprocess_data()
    # FIX: Using the fully qualified path MLDatasets.MNIST.traindata() to
    ensure compatibility
    # across different MLDatasets.jl versions and resolve the
    UndefVarError.
    # traindata() returns (features, labels). We restructure to get only
    the features (imgs).
    imgs, _ = MLDatasets.MNIST.traindata()

    # Flatten images from 28x28xN to 784xN
    X = reshape(imgs, IMAGE_SIZE, :)

    # Normalize pixel values to [0, 1] and convert to Float32
    X = Float32.(X ./ 255.0)
```

```julia
    # Create DataLoader for mini-batch training
    data_loader = Flux.DataLoader(X, batchsize=BATCH_SIZE, shuffle=true)

    return data_loader
end

# --- 2. VAE Model Definition ---

# Define the VAE structure to hold the encoder and decoder parts
struct VAE
    encoder::Chain
    decoder::Chain
    z_mean_layer::Dense
    z_log_var_layer::Dense
end

# A constructor to build the VAE model
function VAE()
    # ENCODER: Maps 784 -> HIDDEN_DIM
    encoder = Chain(
        Dense(IMAGE_SIZE, HIDDEN_DIM, relu),
        Dense(HIDDEN_DIM, HIDDEN_DIM, relu)
    )

    # LATENT LAYERS: Output the mean and log-variance
    z_mean_layer = Dense(HIDDEN_DIM, LATENT_DIM)
    z_log_var_layer = Dense(HIDDEN_DIM, LATENT_DIM)

    # DECODER: Maps LATENT_DIM -> HIDDEN_DIM -> 784 (sigmoid output
    for pixels)
    decoder = Chain(
        Dense(LATENT_DIM, HIDDEN_DIM, relu),
        Dense(HIDDEN_DIM, HIDDEN_DIM, relu),
        Dense(HIDDEN_DIM, IMAGE_SIZE, sigmoid) # Sigmoid activation for [0,
        1] output
    )

    return VAE(encoder, decoder, z_mean_layer, z_log_var_layer)
end
```

```julia
# --- 3. Reparameterization Trick (Sampling) ---

"""
Implements the reparameterization trick: z = mu + sigma * epsilon
where epsilon is standard normal noise.
"""
function reparameterize(mu::AbstractArray, log_var::AbstractArray)
    # 1. Calculate standard deviation (sigma) from log-variance
    sigma = exp.(0.5f0 .* log_var)

    # 2. Sample epsilon from standard normal (same shape as mu)
    epsilon = randn(Float32, size(mu))

    # 3. Calculate latent vector z
    z = mu + sigma .* epsilon
    return z
end

# --- 4. Forward Pass Definition ---

# Define how data flows through the VAE
function (vae::VAE)(x)
    # Encode input to get features
    h = vae.encoder(x)

    # Get latent parameters
    mu = vae.z_mean_layer(h)
    log_var = vae.z_log_var_layer(h)

    # Sample latent vector z using reparameterization trick
    z = reparameterize(mu, log_var)

    # Decode z to get reconstruction
    reconstruction = vae.decoder(z)

    return reconstruction, mu, log_var
end
```

```julia
# --- 5. Custom VAE Loss Function ---

"""
Calculates the VAE loss: Reconstruction Loss + BETA * KL Divergence Loss.
"""
function vae_loss(x, reconstruction, mu, log_var)
    # ------------------
    # 1. Reconstruction Loss (BCE)
    reconstruction_loss = mean(logitbinarycrossentropy(reconstruction, x))

    # ------------------
    # 2. KL Divergence Loss
    # Analytical formula for KL(q(z|x) || P(z)) where P(z) is N(0, I):
    # $$-0.5 \sum (1 + \log \sigma^2 - \mu^2 - \sigma^2)$$
    kl_loss = -0.5f0 .* sum(1.0f0 .+ log_var .- mu.^2 .- exp.(log_
var), dims=1)

    # Average KL loss over the batch
    kl_loss = mean(kl_loss)

    # ------------------
    # 3. Total VAE Loss (ELBO)
    total_loss = reconstruction_loss + BETA * kl_loss

    return total_loss, reconstruction_loss, kl_loss
end

# --- 6. Training Loop ---

function train_vae()
    println("--- VAE Execution Started ---") # Added for debugging flow
    # Load data
    data_loader = load_and_preprocess_data()

    # Initialize VAE model and optimizer
    vae_model = VAE()
    optimizer = ADAM(LEARNING_RATE)
```

```julia
# Flux needs parameters extracted for the optimization step
params = Flux.params(vae_model.encoder, vae_model.decoder,
                    vae_model.z_mean_layer, vae_model.z_log_var_layer)

# Start training
println("\n--- Starting VAE Training ---")

for epoch in 1:EPOCHS
    local total_epoch_loss = 0.0f0
    local total_reconstruction_loss = 0.0f0
    local total_kl_loss = 0.0f0
    local num_batches = 0

    for x_batch in data_loader
        # Ensure batch data is Float32
        x_batch = Float32.(x_batch)

        # Gradient calculation
        gs = Flux.gradient(params) do
            reconstruction, mu, log_var = vae_model(x_batch)

            # Calculate all three losses
            loss, recon_loss, kl_loss = vae_loss(x_batch,
            reconstruction, mu, log_var)

            # Accumulate losses for logging
            total_epoch_loss += loss
            total_reconstruction_loss += recon_loss
            total_kl_loss += kl_loss
            num_batches += 1

            return loss
        end

        # Update model parameters
        train!(optimizer, params, gs)
    end
```

```julia
        # Calculate average losses for the epoch
        avg_loss = total_epoch_loss / num_batches
        avg_recon_loss = total_reconstruction_loss / num_batches
        avg_kl_loss = total_kl_loss / num_batches

        # Use @sprintf for formatted output
        println("Epoch $epoch/$EPOCHS | Total Loss: $(@sprintf("%.4f", avg_
        loss)) | Recon Loss: $(@sprintf("%.4f", avg_recon_loss)) | KL Loss:
        $(@sprintf("%.4f", avg_kl_loss))")
    end

    println("--- Training Complete ---")

    # Return the trained model for sampling/generation
    return vae_model
end

# --- 7. Sampling/Generation Function (Optional/Verification) ---

"""
Generates a new image by sampling from the latent space and running the
decoder.
"""
function generate_sample(vae_model::VAE)
    # 1. Sample a random vector z from the standard normal
    distribution N(0, I)
    z_sample = randn(Float32, LATENT_DIM, 1)

    # 2. Pass z through the decoder
    generated_image_vector = vae_model.decoder(z_sample)

    # 3. Reshape the 784x1 vector back to 28x28 image
    generated_image = reshape(generated_image_vector, 28, 28)

    return generated_image
end
```

```julia
# --- 8. Visualization Function (NEW) ---

"""
Visualizes and saves the 28x28 matrix as a PNG file using Plots.jl.
"""
function save_image(matrix::AbstractMatrix, filename::String)
    # Create a heatmap plot of the matrix. We use grayscale and hide axes.
    p = heatmap(matrix,
                aspect_ratio=:equal,
                axis=nothing,
                c=:grays,
                yflip=false, # Necessary to prevent image from being
                flipped vertically
                size=(300, 300),
                title="Generated MNIST Digit")

    savefig(p, filename)
    println("Saved generated image to $filename")
end

# --- Main Execution (Now runs automatically when included or run
directly) ---

try
    global trained_vae = train_vae()

    # Test generation capability
    println("\nGenerating and saving 5 sample images:")
    for i in 1:5
        sample_matrix = generate_sample(trained_vae)
        filename = @sprintf("generated_sample_%d.png", i)

        # Call the new save function
        save_image(sample_matrix, filename)
    end
```

```julia
catch e
    println("An error occurred during execution: ", e)
    # Updated dependency list
    println("Ensure you have installed the required Julia packages: Flux,
    MLDatasets, Printf, Statistics, Random, and Plots.")
end
```

The first interesting part of the code is the way you create the VAE. In Python we used a *class*, whereas in Julia we use a *struct* for create the VAE.

Structs in Julia are immutable structures used to define composite datatypes that group related data together. In our case, they are used to relate all the components of the variational autoencoder. The encoder and decoder are indicated as a `Chain` type, which is used to connect the encoder and decoder functions.

`z_mean_layer` and `z_log_var_layer` are dense layer types and are calculated by the layer of the neural network.

The other important function is `reparametrize`, which is used to incorporate the *reparameterization trick*. It used to calculate the *mean* and the *log variance* of the data and to produce the sample latent vector Z, ensuring the network remains differentiable.

To train the network, you use `Flux.gradient`, which calculates the `Flux.train!` gradient.

The Denoising Variational Autoencoder in Julia

This section explains how to write a denoise variational autoencoder in Julia, similarly to what you did in Python. It involves a function that adds noise to the data. The implementation is shown in Listing 7-7.

Listing 7-7. The Denoising Variational Autoencoder in Julia

```julia
using Flux
using Flux: train!, mse, binarycrossentropy
using MLDatasets
using Statistics: mean
using Random
using Printf
using Plots
```

```julia
# --- Configuration ---
const LATENT_DIM = 10     # Dimensionality of the latent space
const IMAGE_SIZE = 28 * 28  # 784 for MNIST (28x28)
const HIDDEN_DIM = 256    # Size of the intermediate dense layers
const EPOCHS = 20
const BATCH_SIZE = 128
const LEARNING_RATE = 0.0005
const BETA = 1.0 # Weight for KL divergence (Beta-VAE concept)
# --- DVAE Configuration ---
const NOISE_FACTOR = 0.15f0 # Standard deviation of Gaussian noise to add
to inputs
# Removed GRADIENT_CLIP_NORM and related import due to persistent
UndefVarError

# --- 1. Data Preparation ---

function load_and_preprocess_data()
    # FIX: Using the fully qualified path MLDatasets.MNIST.traindata() to
    ensure compatibility
    # across different MLDatasets.jl versions and resolve the
    UndefVarError.
    # traindata() returns (features, labels). We restructure to get only
    the features (imgs).
    imgs, _ = MLDatasets.MNIST.traindata()

    # Flatten images from 28x28xN to 784xN
    X = reshape(imgs, IMAGE_SIZE, :)

    # Normalize pixel values to [0, 1] and convert to Float32
    X = Float32.(X ./ 255.0)

    # Create DataLoader for mini-batch training
    data_loader = Flux.DataLoader(X, batchsize=BATCH_SIZE, shuffle=true)

    println("Data loaded and preprocessed. Training data size: ", size(X))
    return data_loader
end
```

```julia
# --- Noise Utility for DVAE ---
"""
Adds Gaussian noise to the input images and clips values to the [0,
1] range.
"""
function add_noise(X::AbstractArray; factor=NOISE_FACTOR)
    # Generate Gaussian noise with standard deviation of 'factor'
    noise = randn(Float32, size(X)) .* factor

    # Add noise to the input
    X_noisy = X .+ noise

    # Clip values to ensure they remain in the valid range [0, 1]
    return clamp.(X_noisy, 0.0f0, 1.0f0)
end

# --- 2. VAE Model Definition ---

# Define the VAE structure to hold the encoder and decoder parts
struct VAE
    encoder::Chain
    decoder::Chain
    z_mean_layer::Dense
    z_log_var_layer::Dense
end

# A constructor to build the VAE model
function VAE()
    # ENCODER: Maps 784 -> HIDDEN_DIM
    encoder = Chain(
        Dense(IMAGE_SIZE, HIDDEN_DIM, relu),
        Dense(HIDDEN_DIM, HIDDEN_DIM, relu)
    )

    # LATENT LAYERS: Output the mean and log-variance
    z_mean_layer = Dense(HIDDEN_DIM, LATENT_DIM)
    z_log_var_layer = Dense(HIDDEN_DIM, LATENT_DIM)
```

```julia
    # DECODER: Maps LATENT_DIM -> HIDDEN_DIM -> 784 (sigmoid output
    for pixels)
    decoder = Chain(
        Dense(LATENT_DIM, HIDDEN_DIM, relu),
        Dense(HIDDEN_DIM, HIDDEN_DIM, relu),
        Dense(HIDDEN_DIM, IMAGE_SIZE, sigmoid) # Sigmoid activation for [0,
        1] output
    )

    return VAE(encoder, decoder, z_mean_layer, z_log_var_layer)
end

# --- 3. Reparameterization Trick (Sampling) ---

"""
Implements the reparameterization trick: z = mu + sigma * epsilon
where epsilon is standard normal noise.
"""
function reparameterize(mu::AbstractArray, log_var::AbstractArray)
    # 1. Calculate standard deviation (sigma) from log-variance
    sigma = exp.(0.5f0 .* log_var)

    # 2. Sample epsilon from standard normal (same shape as mu)
    epsilon = randn(Float32, size(mu))

    # 3. Calculate latent vector z
    z = mu + sigma .* epsilon
    return z
end

# --- 4. Forward Pass Definition ---

# Define how data flows through the VAE
# NOTE: For DVAE, 'x' here represents the *NOISY* input being passed
through the encoder.
function (vae::VAE)(x)
    # Encode input to get features
    h = vae.encoder(x)
```

```julia
    # Get latent parameters
    mu = vae.z_mean_layer(h)
    log_var = vae.z_log_var_layer(h)

    # Sample latent vector z using reparameterization trick
    z = reparameterize(mu, log_var)

    # Decode z to get reconstruction
    reconstruction = vae.decoder(z)

    return reconstruction, mu, log_var
end

# --- 5. Custom VAE Loss Function ---

"""
Calculates the VAE loss: Reconstruction Loss + BETA * KL Divergence Loss.
NOTE: 'x' is the CLEAN TARGET image for the reconstruction loss.
"""
function vae_loss(x, reconstruction, mu, log_var)

    # -------------------
    # 1. Reconstruction Loss (BCE)
    # Using binarycrossentropy as reconstruction is already a probability
    (sigmoid output)
    reconstruction_loss = mean(binarycrossentropy(reconstruction, x))

    # -------------------
    # 2. KL Divergence Loss
    # Analytical formula for KL(q(z|x) || P(z)) where P(z) is N(0, I):
    # $$-0.5 \sum (1 + \log \sigma^2 - \mu^2 - \sigma^2)$$
    kl_loss = -0.5f0 .* sum(1.0f0 .+ log_var .- mu.^2 .- exp.(log_
    var), dims=1)

    # Average KL loss over the batch
    kl_loss = mean(kl_loss)
```

```julia
    # ------------------
    # 3. Total VAE Loss (ELBO)
    total_loss = reconstruction_loss + BETA * kl_loss

    return total_loss, reconstruction_loss, kl_loss
end

# --- 6. Training Loop ---

function train_vae()
    println("--- Denoising VAE Execution Started ---")
    # Load clean data
    data_loader = load_and_preprocess_data()

    # Initialize VAE model and optimizer
    vae_model = VAE()
    optimizer = ADAM(LEARNING_RATE)

    # Flux needs parameters extracted for the optimization step
    params = Flux.params(vae_model.encoder, vae_model.decoder,
                         vae_model.z_mean_layer, vae_model.z_log_var_layer)

    # Start training
    println("\n--- Starting Denoising VAE Training ---")

    for epoch in 1:EPOCHS
        local total_epoch_loss = 0.0f0
        local total_reconstruction_loss = 0.0f0
        local total_kl_loss = 0.0f0
        local num_batches = 0

        # x_clean_batch is the target image (y)
        for x_clean_batch in data_loader
            # Ensure batch data is Float32
            x_clean_batch = Float32.(x_clean_batch)

            # --- DVAE Step: Generate Noisy Input ---
            x_noisy_batch = add_noise(x_clean_batch)
```

```
            # Gradient calculation
            gs = Flux.gradient(params) do
                # VAE forward pass uses the NOISY input
                reconstruction, mu, log_var = vae_model(x_noisy_batch)

                # Loss calculation uses the CLEAN input as the target (x)
                loss, recon_loss, kl_loss = vae_loss(x_clean_batch,
                reconstruction, mu, log_var)

                # Accumulate losses for logging
                total_epoch_loss += loss
                total_reconstruction_loss += recon_loss
                total_kl_loss += kl_loss
                num_batches += 1

                return loss
            end

            # Update model parameters using raw gradients (stable
            with low LR)
            train!(optimizer, params, gs)
        end

        # Calculate average losses for the epoch
        avg_loss = total_epoch_loss / num_batches
        avg_recon_loss = total_reconstruction_loss / num_batches
        avg_kl_loss = total_kl_loss / num_batches

        # Use @sprintf for formatted output
        println("Epoch $epoch/$EPOCHS | Total Loss: $(@sprintf("%.4f", avg_
        loss)) | Recon Loss: $(@sprintf("%.4f", avg_recon_loss)) | KL Loss:
        $(@sprintf("%.4f", avg_kl_loss))")
    end

    println("--- Training Complete ---")

    # Return the trained model for sampling/generation
    return vae_model
end
```

```julia
# --- 7. Sampling/Generation Function (Optional/Verification) ---

"""
Generates a new image by sampling from the latent space and running the
decoder.
"""
function generate_sample(vae_model::VAE)
    # 1. Sample a random vector z from the standard normal
    distribution N(0, I)
    z_sample = randn(Float32, LATENT_DIM, 1)

    # 2. Pass z through the decoder
    generated_image_vector = vae_model.decoder(z_sample)

    # 3. Reshape the 784x1 vector back to 28x28 image
    generated_image = reshape(generated_image_vector, 28, 28)

    # Print max and min values to verify the output range [0, 1]
    println("\nGenerated Sample Stats: Max=$(maximum(generated_image)),
    Min=$(minimum(generated_image))")

    return generated_image
end

# --- 8. Visualization Function ---

"""
Visualizes and saves the 28x28 matrix as a PNG file using Plots.jl.
"""
function save_image(matrix::AbstractMatrix, filename::String)
    # Create a heatmap plot of the matrix. We use grayscale and hide axes.
    # We explicitly choose the 'gr' backend for headless/stable
    environments.
    Plots.gr()
    p = heatmap(matrix,
                aspect_ratio=:equal,
                axis=nothing,
                c=:grays,
```

```julia
                yflip=false, # Necessary to prevent image from being
                flipped vertically
                size=(300, 300),
                title="Generated MNIST Digit")

    savefig(p, filename)
    println("Saved generated image to $filename")
end

# --- Main Execution (Now runs automatically when included or run
directly) ---

try
    global trained_vae = train_vae()

    # Test generation capability
    println("\nGenerating and saving 5 sample images:")
    for i in 1:5
        sample_matrix = generate_sample(trained_vae)
        filename = @sprintf("generated_sample_%d.png", i)

        # Call the new save function
        save_image(sample_matrix, filename)
    end
catch e
    println("An error occurred during execution: ", e)
    # Updated dependency list
    println("Ensure you have installed the required Julia packages: Flux,
    MLDatasets, Printf, Statistics, Random, and Plots.")
end
```

The main difference between the convolutional variational autoencoder and the denoising variational autoencoder is the add_noise function, which is used to add the noise to the data and allow the variational autoencoder to learn the data with the noise.

The function adds Gaussian noise to the data by creating a *noisy batch* of the data. This is create with this line: codex_noisy_batch = add_noise(x_clean_batch). This will add the noise to the original data and allow the VAEs to learn the data. This will make the VAEs learn how to clean the data and reconstruct the image without the data.

Looking Ahead and Conclusion

Up to now, you have been learning about models used for generative artificial intelligence. This area of the AI is way more complex than the LLMs. LLMs are based on transformers and this is just one for the architectures of the generative artificial intelligence.

This field is a huge one, and it's evolving day by day. Artificial generative intelligence brings great power, and of course great responsibility. We live in an era of social media, and with that comes a lot of misinformation. This is sometimes driven but what is called *deepfakes*, which are artificial intelligence artifacts. In many case, we cannot recognize any more what is real and what is fake without deep analysis.

Like anything else, how this is used makes all the difference of the world. We can use it to further science and medical detection, or use it to lie to, foment distrust, and manipulate people.

In conclusion, this book is only the starting point of any journey about generative artificial intelligence. As Steve Jobs said, "Stay hungry, stay foolish." If you want get better, continue to learn and explore this fascinating field of AI.

H

T

U

GPSR Compliance
The European Union's (EU) General Product Safety Regulation (GPSR) is a set
of rules that requires consumer products to be safe and our obligations to
ensure this.

If you have any concerns about our products, you can contact us on

ProductSafety@springernature.com

In case Publisher is established outside the EU, the EU authorized
representative is:

Springer Nature Customer Service Center GmbH
Europaplatz 3
69115 Heidelberg, Germany